FEARLESS

Abundant Life through Infinite Love

Margaret Mary Vasquez, LPCC-S

Scripture texts in this work taken from the *New American Bible*, ©1991, 1986, and 1970 by the Confraternity of Christian Doctrine, Washington, DC. Used by permission. All rights reserved.

Sacred Heart Healing Ministries
P.O. Box 724
Steubenville, OH 43952

© 2021 by Margaret Mary Vasquez

All rights reserved. No part of this publication may be reproduced, distributed, or transmitted in any form or by any means, including photocopying, recording, or other electronic or mechanical methods without the prior written permission of the publisher except for brief quotations embodied in critical reviews.

Printed in the United States.

ISBN: 9798774323111

In memory of Joseph Wendler

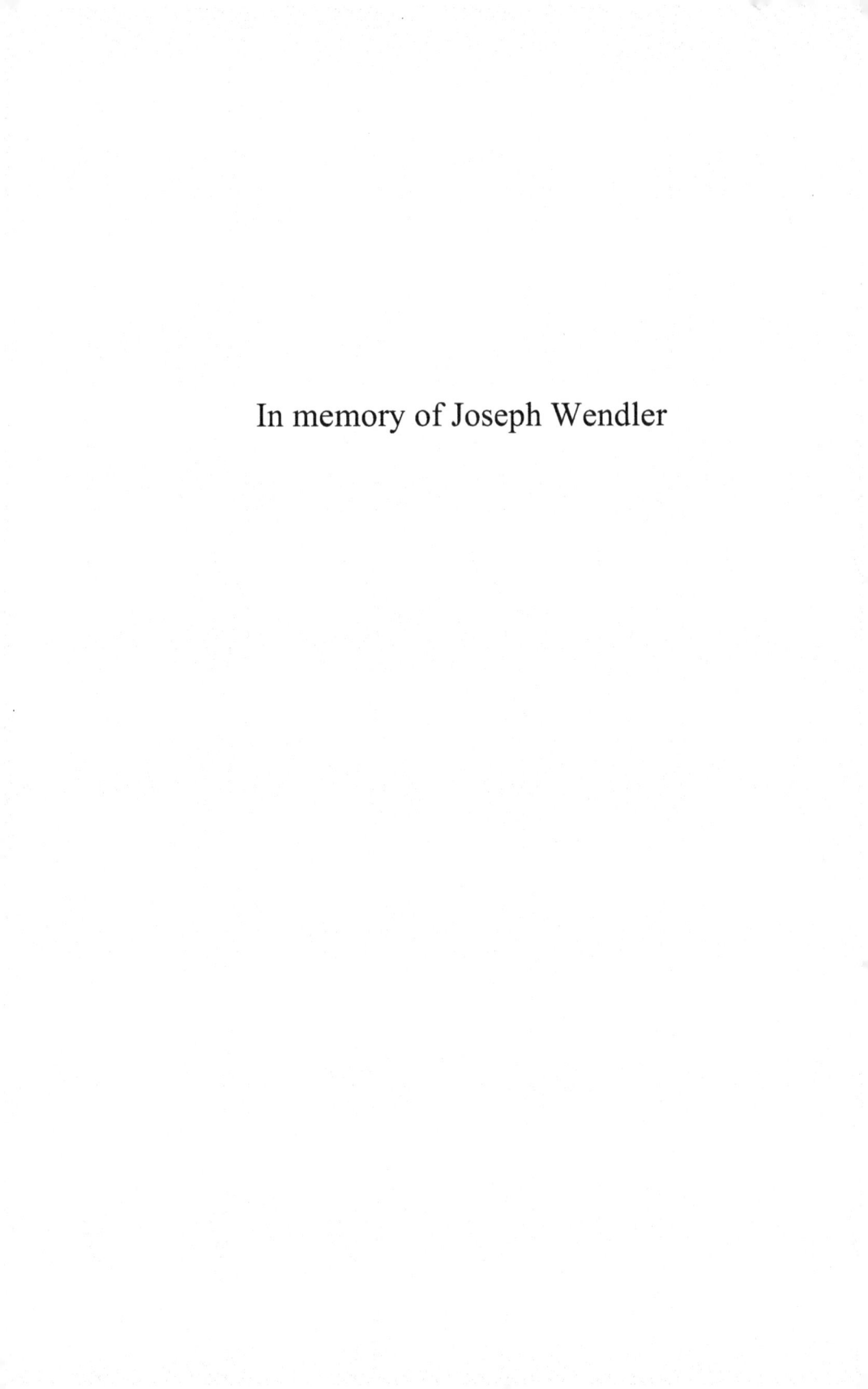

CONTENTS

Foreword	vii
Preface	ix
Acknowledgements	xi
Introduction	1
How to Use This Book	7
Connection Overview	11
Connection to God	19
Chosen for Divine Intimacy	23
Known by God	27
Valued by God	31
Prayer	35
God Provides Boundaries	43
God's Openness	49
Openness with God	53
Knowing God	59
Valuing God	63
Embracing God's Boundaries	67
Suffering	73
Powerlessness	77
Going Deeper	83

Connection to Self	87
Knowing Myself	95
Valuing Myself	101
My Boundaries for Myself	107
Openness with Myself	113
Body, Mind, Spirit	119
Connection to Others	125
Boundaries for Others	131
Respecting the Boundaries of Others	137
Openness with Others	143
Openness from Others	149
Valuing & Being Valued	155
Knowing & Being Known	161
Healthy Communication	167
Navigating Relational Struggles	173
Pseudo-Connection	177
Conclusion	181
Special Note	183
Appendix	185
Notes	193
Resources	197

FOREWORD

I was reassigned to Franciscan University in Steubenville, Ohio in March of 2020, one week before the outbreak of Covid-19. Some months later I was introduced to Margaret Vasquez through a pastoral situation and I had the opportunity of ministering on a retreat she was leading where I saw the application of these connection principles in a retreat format. I realized that a whole new arena of developing the "culture of connection" is possible. Now a larger number of individuals can magnanimously benefit through the book you hold in your hands. While true that an individual who is severely traumatized may still need treatment even after making retreats of connection and integration, I am convinced that many more people can experience healing from disintegrating pain and come to know the liberating peace and joy of a new life of fearlessness.

"Write down the vision clearly upon the tablets, so that one can read it readily. For the vision still has its time, presses on to fulfillment, and will not disappoint" (Habakkuk 2:2-3). Margaret's clear vision and conviction presented in this book relates to a threefold culture of connection resulting in a wonderful integration in the human person and relationships. The present negative conditions in our society illustrate a devastating destruction and disintegration in our culture, also within the Church. There needs to be a new culture, a new way of living, in the Church and in our society. Margaret has taken up the challenge by presenting a new culture of fearlessness through connection, integration, and compassion to bring about integration, renewal and restoration.

As a priest for more than 50 years, I have seen the paralyzing effects of the wounds people carry. Broken hearts lead to lives of stagnation, scrupulosity, and turmoil. It does not need to be so. The Lord's infinite merciful love sets the captives free from the shackles of fear. You are so deeply loved. Join the revolution!

Rev. David Tickerhoof, TOR
Franciscan University of Steubenville, Pastoral Associate

PREFACE

Many years ago, I noticed that healthy connections to God, self, and others are the foundation of peace and fulfillment in life. Without these connections, we perpetuate lies in our minds that become the basis for our self-talk and the ways we relate to others. These lies chip away at our ability to perceive and receive the truth of God's love for us and leave us feeling like he is far away. With a faith rendered full of holes, we are anxiety ridden and depressed; we find ourselves perpetuating a cycle of disconnection within ourselves and with those around us. The remedy is simple. Four scripture-based essentials (respect for boundaries, inherent value as God's children, recognition of the goodness with which he made us, and openness) are all that is necessary for healthy relating to God, self, and others. These essentials lead to the abundant life Jesus came to give us. This revelation led me to write this book. I encourage you to pray through it and allow the Lord to minister the truth of his love to you.

ACKNOWLEDGEMENTS

I am deeply appreciative of those who gave generously of their time to read this book along the way and give feedback and assistance. In particular, I am grateful to Father David Tickerhoof, TOR, Deacon Mark Erste, and Cindy Welker for your encouragement. Thank you to Catherine Poulin and Isaiah Ballard for your technical assistance. Linda Craig, your copy editing, cover artwork, and cheerleading has been a precious gift. Bev Richards, my tireless sounding board, many thanks. Put it on my tab. I also want to thank you, each reader, for seeking to know more fully the truth that you are loved. Knowing that there are people like you has given me the courage and motivation to write this book.

INTRODUCTION

I'm writing this in the time of lockdown during the coronavirus pandemic. We are being bombarded daily with dire forecasts about the connectedness of humanity. If we carry the virus, we are told we risk making others sick. Social media is plastered with posts and memes that speak of people longing to once again relate closely. Post after post gives people tips on how to cope with the loss of social contact. We long for connection. The pandemic of disconnection is far more deadly and far less recognized in our world than any virus.

As a licensed professional clinical counselor and trauma therapist, I've practiced intensive trauma therapy with clients of all ages for the past 15+ years. Time and again, I've witnessed that the deepest and most damaging human experiences come from fractures in connection. These fractures leave people isolated, their ability to relate to themselves and others, broken. I've been blessed to practice and further develop a highly effective method of treatment. The approach treats the traumas first. After the trauma is healed, the need for healthy connection invariably comes to the forefront, but knowing how to build these connections is not always a given. I have watched people expend great fear-based energy trying to control rather than to truly connect, exacerbating their own suffering and the suffering of those around them.

For more than a decade of providing therapy, the most profoundly positive and healing experiences people have shared with me are times they felt connected to God, to others, or to themselves. Over and over again regardless of age, gender, socio-economic background, cognitive level, or any other factor, connection, true, authentic, healthy connection, is the antithesis of trauma. Connection is what we are made for and the climate in which we all flourish.

Real communion, I came to understand, is consistently fostered by boundaries, recognition of value and acceptance, and being seen and heard as a unique and precious individual. These form the core of connection. They flow throughout sacred scripture and synergistically provide the sense of safety necessary for vulnerability and trust. When these ways of being are operating, people are truly able to perceive and receive each other in love, peace, and joy. These same factors are necessary for a healthy relationship to self and to the Lord, as well. When we know the four elements of healthy connection and why and how they fit and work together, we are able to build on solid ground and to navigate compassionately when relationships become challenging. Without this knowledge, we can easily lose peace and focus.

Accepting the intimacy of the Blessed Trinity residing in us, we start from a place of fullness with our connection needs met to overflowing. We are perfectly known, valued, and protected by our all-loving, omnipotent God. His perfect love dispels and replaces our fear. (1 John 4:18) It is essential, and commonly most difficult, for us to accept and imitate such love as we relate to ourselves. The healthier our self-talk and integration of his love, the safer we feel, the less others are viewed as threat or competition, and the more his love flows through us to others. That unshakeable assurance we have in God's love, transforms our hearts and minds. Such fearlessness flows outward into every aspect of our lives. It is the superabundance of God's infinite compassion for us that is the truest way to find both sanity and sanctity. This is that same Deep Well from which the saints drank. He is no less available to us when we make ourselves available to him. Much of the focus of therapy is often about identifying lies we believe about ourselves which stem from painful experiences. While this can be a crucial step to healing from the past, it's imperative for us to adopt a new way of relating for the future. We must begin to relate to ourselves, God, and others the way the Lord does for the truth of his love to transform our minds and lead us into his abundant life.

Jesus' identity was firmly rooted in being the beloved Son of the Father (Connection to God). He thoroughly internalized that identity (Connection to Self) and he related to others in a way that allowed the love of his Father to flow through himself to them in deep compassion (Connection to Others). Connection to God, to self, and to others is the ever-deepening work of a lifetime. It is not bad news that we haven't arrived, but rather something to embrace. It's not that we aren't good enough or are still broken if we have room for formation in these areas. Rather, it's the profound reality that God is infinite and being permeated by his all-loving presence is a process. There is always more of him – more love, more peace, more joy. This is really good news!

As I dug into writing this book and was looking for scriptures for each section, scales fell from my eyes. I had previously seen the four connection principles of boundaries, valued, being known, and openness as a ubiquitous pattern, and mentally and spiritually sound. What struck me was that all of scripture is bursting with these concepts, too. I called a friend and told her my find. Without missing a beat she responded, "That makes sense. Scripture is all relationship". My jaw dropped. That's it! These connection principles are how the Lord relates to us and how he teaches us to relate, as well. Is it any wonder that they lead to wholeness and freedom?

HOW TO USE THIS BOOK

You have a variety of options when it comes to using this book. There is no right or wrong, complete or incomplete way to do so. If you're a perfectionist, like I can be, you may need to hear it's not work or a school assignment. It's simply a tool. Hopefully, you will find this tool to be useful as you grow towards a life of deeper fulfillment and peace in holiness and wholeness. Because it is a tool, you may use more or less of it than others do. We are all so different, with different needs, different amounts of free time, and in different places in our own formation needs. You may have more or less familiarity with this type of information and so may want to plunge in more deeply right away or desire to read through the content first in order to become familiar with it. You may pack it away and pull it out years later and find you approach it in an entirely different way given where you are along your journey. I'll explain why each of the portions within the sections are provided for you, so you can decide what is most helpful for you at this time.

- Quotes – each section begins with a quote, to help you get into the frame of mind for that section.
- Paragraphs of Explanation – comprise each section and provide you with an introduction to the main thought being covered.
- Questions for Reflection/Discussion – these are meant to help you apply the content personally, so you can begin to think about your life in terms of connection and see how the pieces align for you. You may choose to work through this on your own, with another, or in a group.
- Prayers – suggested prayers are included to invite the Lord's grace into your life and to remind you this is fundamentally his work. He has created us and is restoring us as he draws us more deeply to himself. Going through this work is meant to help us enter into his healing presence, which is always at work in our lives.
- Action steps – these are provided in case you are looking for a way to implement what was covered in the explanation. People have different learning styles. Action steps can be useful, especially for those who are hands-on learners.

- Journal Prompts – each section also provides a thought to consider for deeper reflection, as a way to dig in and draw even more deeply on God's healing and grace. If you aren't a fan of journaling, you may want to consider the content from this area as you exercise, commute to work or school, or do chores. That is, you're still welcome to use the content from these sections, even if you don't choose to write down your thoughts. In this case, it really is the thought that counts.

- Scriptures – a number of passages from sacred scripture are provided for meditation for those who would like to use this workbook as a tool in their prayer time. They are to help you understand the correlation between holiness and wholeness in your daily life and may help you understand more deeply God's covenant as the blueprint of true connection.

- Appendix – this is included to provide extra material pertaining to the concepts in this book, should you desire to go deeper into the provided content.

CONNECTION OVERVIEW

...in him all things hold together

– Colossians 1:17

What is so important about connection and why pair it together with the concept of holiness? We don't have to look far to see how God regards community. He models it for us in the Holy Trinity. We see their love, unity and order in relationship to each other. Each knows, values and respects the others. There is diversity and perfect unity. When God the Father sent his Son into the world, Jesus did only what he saw the Father do (John 5:19). After his Ascension Jesus sent the Holy Spirit, the Spirit of adoption, to bring us into the family of God as brothers and sisters; sons and daughters of our heavenly Father. The Spirit gives us the power to live the life of God. He animates us to make God visible, to incarnate God in our lives.

So much does God desire to be connected to us and for us to be connected to each other, that he condescends to humble himself so far as to transform bread and wine into his body and blood. He remains with us in all the tabernacles of the world, even enduring coldness and indifference, to be with us always so we might know we are never alone. Charity and unity are intimately tied to the Eucharist. His love for us feeds our hunger for union with him. The more we consciously and intentionally relate to ourselves and each other with such compassion, the more we draw nearer to him and each other, as we sing in the second verse of "Thou, Who at Thy First Eucharist Did Pray":

> For all your Church, O Lord, we intercede;
>
> O make our lack of charity to cease;
>
> Draw us the nearer each to each, we plead,
>
> By drawing all to you, O prince of peace.[1]

In the story of the prodigal son (Luke 15:11-32), when the older brother complains about the younger son's return, he tries to disassociate himself from his overindulgent brother. He says to his father, "But when this son of yours who has squandered your property with prostitutes comes home, you kill the fatted calf for him!"(Luke 15:30) The father made it a point to remind the older son of his relationship to his brother: "But now we must celebrate and rejoice, because *your brother* was dead and has come to life again; he was lost and has been found." (Luke 15:32) The father sought to reconcile the older son to himself, and to bring him wholeness in his relationship with his brother.

It is very important to the Lord that we have communion with him and with each other. God is not just the father of each of us; he is *our* father. We are siblings. 'Father' is a title that not only defines our relationship to him, but also to each other. He is the hub and we are the spokes on the wheel. As we draw closer to him, we draw closer to one another. He desires to draw us all to himself and to each other.

Being united is essential to the nature of the Most Blessed Trinity. It is who they are. It is not an activity. That is to say, their unity is about being, not about doing. Because it is who they are, it is how they relate. It is not a tactic or strategic approach. There is no ulterior motive. Relating in healthy connection to ourselves and others is both holy and fosters wholeness. It is imitation of God. He set before us life and death and longs for us to choose life, because such things draw us more deeply into the fullness of how he made us to be and the joy of the life he has for us. The Greek word *teleios* means both wholeness and holiness. Living in healthy, loving, respectful connection calls us to growth on human and spiritual levels. It helps us to make our love of God manifest in our own lives and to those around us.

It stands to reason we are the most fulfilled and at peace when life is lived the way God intended. St. John Paul II's encyclical, *Fides et Ratio*[2], tells us that faith and reason are not just compatible, but essential to a life well-lived. Science reveals to us that God wired into our physical being a need for social connection. In his TED Talk about social connection[3], neuroscientist Matthew Lieberman, Ph. D., tells us that connection to each other even impacts our physical health on a day-to-day basis.

The final aspect of connection is personal integration, connection to self. It's not something we talk about much, but it is something impacting all of us constantly. St. Thomas Aquinas said, "What is received is received according to the mode of the receiver."[4] Our connection to ourselves is this mode. If we are patient, kind, and understanding toward ourselves, it is going to be much easier for us to relate to our neighbor in the same way. Likewise, if we believe we are lovable, it will be much easier for us to believe God loves us. In fact, I've seen time and again that most of us don't sin because of faulty theology, but a very erroneous 'me-ology'. That is, our lack of acceptance of ourselves and our belief that we are not worthy of the Lord's intense, intimate, personal passionate desire for each one of us is what leaves us worshipping all sorts of other gods, in an attempt to medicate our pain, loneliness, and emptiness. We must begin to shift how we see ourselves in order to begin to believe the truth of how God sees us. When we consciously and intentionally stand under the truth of how God sees us, we begin to more fully understand the depth of his passion and compassion for us. Only this will truly satisfy the longing of our hearts.

All three of these dimensions of connection – connection to God, self, and others – are crucial for wholeness and holiness in our lives, much like the legs of a tripod provide balance. Connection to God is the perfection of intimacy and provides us with the essential basis for being truly known and accepted. In this way, we have a firm foundation for self-knowledge and self-acceptance. Then, in truly loving ourselves, we can best be conduits of his love to others. It makes no sense to be harsh and demanding with ourselves for most of our waking hours and then expect the comparatively small amount of time spent in listening to God's voice to renew our minds.

Questions for Reflection and Discussion

1. In what way do you experience the most connection in your life currently?
2. In what way would you most like to grow in connection?
3. Which area of connection (God, self, others) is the easiest for you? Why?
4. Which area of connection (God, self, others) is the most difficult for you? Why?

Prayer

Let's pray the *Our Father* together, considering especially the reality of our connection to each other as brothers and sisters in our heavenly Father.

Action Step

Pay attention to your positive interactions with others and how you are a conduit for the power of God flowing through you to minister to others, even in simple ways like a smile, a greeting, listening, or a small act of service

Journaling/Further Reflection

Spend some time reflecting on the Lord's invitation to you for deeper intimacy in his life. Ask the Lord to share with you what he wants you to know about this and then note what stirs in your heart.

Scriptures for Meditation

Psalm 133:1

John 17:20-26

Romans 8:15

Ephesians 4:3

Ephesians 4:16

CONNECTION TO GOD

Thou hast made us for thyself, O Lord, and our heart is restless until it finds its rest in thee.

– St. Augustine of Hippo

The *Catechism of the Catholic Church* teaches that the Eucharist is the "source and summit of the Christian life."[1] Jesus is the bread of life. He is the food for which we are made. What does food do? It nourishes us, gives us energy. Good food makes us healthy, bad food makes us sick, poisoned food can even kill us, but without food we would die a painful death. Fundamentally, food satisfies us. We eat so that we can live.

What does it mean to say that the Eucharist is, "the source and summit of the Christian life," if not to say that Communion – deep, personal, intimate connection with God – is essential to being healthy and vivacious rather than sick, malnourished, and dying. If our connection to God is only in physical reception of the Eucharist and not in spiritual intimacy, then we are missing out on that for which our soul is ultimately yearning and seeking. He has so much more to offer us than for us to just go through the motions of receiving him. He longs for us to unite ourselves to him fully in every aspect of our person. He wants every facet of us to be nourished and healthy.

We are made for healthy food, but if we do not have access to it, we are still driven to eat. Eventually, we'll settle for chips, a candy bar, or a soda because our hunger demands to be fed. If we don't make planful and intentional choices, we will run the risk of making impulsive ones. It is the same way with being fed spiritually, emotionally and relationally. We are made for God who is infinite. Only he can fully satisfy our hunger. If we aren't feeding on him in all of these ways, who or what are we consuming? Whatever or whomever it is, it won't fill us because it wasn't made to, no matter how hard we or they try.

If we treat the spiritual life – our communion with God – as dessert or a side dish, nothing will be smooth, peaceful, or fulfilling for very long. Ultimately, we'll be making unrealistic demands of our very nature as we seek to be patient, understanding and committed to others. We have to be fed first. We cannot give what we don't have. To try to do so is like jumping off a building and expecting to fly. If we are hoping to be fed by others, we are setting ourselves, and them, up for an impossible task that is bound to end in stagnation, dependence, resentment, or destruction.

Questions for Reflection and Discussion

1. In what way(s) do you feel like you're running on empty – emotionally, spiritually or relationally malnourished?
2. In what way(s) do you find yourself trying to be fed elsewhere? How is that working out?
3. In what new way(s) can you allow the Lord to feed you?

Prayer

Lord, we are made for you and you generously empty your infinite self for us at every moment. Please bring us to deeper awareness of our need for you and your desire to be our fulfillment. We thank you for longing to answer this prayer beyond our wildest hopes. In Jesus' name we pray. Amen.

Action Step

Before you check your phone in the morning or get out of bed, ask the Lord to fill you with himself and spend a couple of minutes receiving his love before your feet even hit the floor.

Journaling/Further Reflection

Ask the Lord to show you in what area(s) you are running without his nourishment and how he wants to be your sustenance so you can start to live your life from a place of fulfillment. Note what he puts on your heart.

Scriptures for Meditation

Luke 18:1

John 14:6

John 15:5-7

1 Thessalonians 5:17

Jude 1:21

CHOSEN FOR DIVINE INTIMACY

It was not you who chose me, but I who chose you…

- John 15:16

God chose each of us individually out of all the possibilities of people to create, redeem, sanctify, and call into relationship with himself for all eternity. I remember hearing that there is a one in 400 quadrillion chance for each one of us to be created. Yet, it wasn't by chance, but by the intentional choice of the Lord of all creation. Not only did he choose for us to exist, but to exist within him and he desires to completely permeate us with his presence. Such an intimate relationship can only be hinted at by the intimacy of marriage.

We are conceived first and foremost in the Holy Trinity and we are members of the Holy Family with Jesus as our brother. Anyone who truly knew and understood this would most certainly choose him, and yet he tells us it was rather he who chose us. Our task is to internalize the fact that we are chosen and the life that results is a life of ever-deepening gratitude and joy.

He longs for us and with him is where we belong. He is the Prince of Peace and we are made for Him. As we accept his choice of us and live ever more fully and deeply as members of his family, we experience his reign over us and are permeated by and become instruments of his peace, bringing others more fully into their citizenship in his Kingdom.

This is the starting point, the foundation. He gave it all, even his life and his Holy Spirit to show us that he will go to any lengths and do all that is necessary to be with us always and forever. Everything else hinges on this foundation, that we were personally selected by he who is all-good, out of his infinite love, that we might be transformed by love and live in union with him.

Every other hope for being chosen pales in comparison to the belonging we have had from the moment of conception. Internalizing and responding to this fact is to be the bottom line of our relationship with him.

Questions for Reflection and Discussion

1. What do you think when you consider the fact that you don't have to try to be chosen, but that you are already chosen by God?
2. How do you feel knowing that bringing the possibility of you to reality was a distinct and intentional choice of God?
3. Does knowing this change how you see yourself? God? Others? Life? If so, how?

Prayer

Heavenly Father, Creator of all things and my Creator, thank you for choosing to bring me into existence to share your life and love for all eternity. Please give me the grace to never forget that fact about myself and to relate to others in a way that acknowledges that same dignity. Amen.

Action Step

Put a note on your bathroom mirror to remind you that God has selected you.

Journaling/Further Reflection

Consider what would be different if you lived completely out of the truth that you are God's choice and jot down what comes to you.

Scriptures for Meditation

Isaiah 43:1

John 15:16

Romans 8:29-30

Ephesians 1:3-4

KNOWN BY GOD

Before I formed you in the womb I knew you...

– Jeremiah 1:5

As we begin to take a look at connection to the Lord, we start with the fact that he deeply and personally knows us. Ideally, we would have had a sense of being known (seen and heard as an individual who is very good) by our parents and caregivers as children. When that happens, it naturally creates a schema in our minds by which we are able to mature more smoothly and with a positive self-concept. The experience of being regarded as an individual who is seen and heard personally as 'very good' (Genesis 1:31), the way God sees us, becomes the basis for how we view ourselves.

For those of us who did not have such an experience as a child, it's never too late. The Lord knows each of us in a deeply intimate way and that's a good thing! He sees each one of us with all the beauty he deposited within us. We each delight his heart in a very special way no one else does or ever can. You are made to reflect an aspect of his magnificence in a way no one ever has or ever will. You are not a number to him. Scripture tells us he has even counted the hairs of our head. He is the most loving father there ever could be. He has called us to be his children. With him as father, it's never too late to have a great childhood.

Oftentimes, we hear or read about having a personal relationship with the Lord. Do we consider he knows us each, personally? That is the starting place. He is the one who has initiated our relationship. "In this is love: not that we have loved God, but that he loved us", as 1 John tells us (1 John 4:10). Imagine how a good parent delights in their newborn or toddler. Such joy is not in what the child can do for them, but simply for whom the child is. God delights in each of us the same way. He sees in us unique characteristics of his own design. His father's heart is filled with love at the sight of each of us.

This is the heart of God. This is the well from which he wants us to draw living waters. The well of his heart is infinite, superabundant and will never run dry. There is always a deeper intimacy he has for each of us and for which he longs. Intimacy with him is the source of deepest fulfillment. He longs for us to experience being known by him. He desires to give us this gift, his love, himself. Learning to draw this living water of his love is a process. Drinking these life-giving waters takes time in prayer and conscious effort. When so much noise clamors around us, it is necessary to remind ourselves of the presence of God so we can be lifted above the noise.

Questions for Reflection and Discussion

1. Is there a way or a place you experience God's love as personal?
2. At what times is it particularly challenging to remember the Lord is with you?
3. Is it difficult for you to believe God sees you as an individual? Why?
4. What is something that draws you into deeper intimacy with God?

Prayer

Pray Psalm 139.

Action Step

Find a way to remind yourself throughout the day of the Lord's presence with you.

Journaling/Further Reflection

Consider how you did or did not feel known as an individual who was very good when you were a child. Invite the Lord into whatever memories come and ask him what he wants you to know. Note what comes to mind.

Scriptures for Meditation

Jeremiah 1:5

Nahum 1:7

Psalm 139

John 10:14

John 10:27

VALUED BY GOD

See what love the Father has bestowed on us that we may be called children of God.

– 1 John 3:1

God's love for us is unlike any other. As covered in the previous section, God created us and so knows us and loves us intimately. Now consider he does so knowing he will always be giving to us far more than we could ever begin to repay, far more than we will even be able to comprehend. He is not just a good father. He is our heavenly Father. He is God and adopts us as his own. This means he chooses us freely, knowing everything about us, good, bad and ugly.

At times we experience circumstantial relationships, like the interaction with a clerk in a store or wait staff in a restaurant. Both parties know the primary purpose for the encounter is an exchange of goods or services. Such times can be transformed into healing and evangelistic encounters when we take the time to truly see and acknowledge the human being before us. We may also experience personal relationships where the message is conveyed that the other is mostly interested in what we can provide them, for example, if someone relates to us for our looks, money, status or because they want us to do something for them. When interpersonal relationships take on a transactional dimension, it can be quite painful. It can leave us feeling treated like an object or as a means to an end. This is the absolute opposite of God and how he relates to us. Rather than giving to us for what he can receive from us, he gives to us desiring our capacity for him to increase so we may receive more and more.

Jesus who is total fullness emptied himself (Philippians 2:7) in order to become one of us. He desired to redeem each of us by his self-sacrificing love, already foreknowing how we would blow it. Not only that, but he chooses to seek us out when we are lost. He is the good shepherd and leaves the ninety-nine to find us as we hear in the Gospel parable (Matthew 18:12-14). His love for us is not transactional or because he needs something from us. He cherishes us as surely as a shepherd would treasure a lost sheep once he found it.

Questions for Reflection and Discussion

1. Recall a time you felt valued for who you are and not for what you could give or do. What stands out about it to you?

2. What image of Jesus helps you to conceptualize his unconditional love for you?

3. What makes it difficult for you to fully accept the fact that God values you for who you are?

Prayer

Heavenly Father, you are the Good Shepherd who seeks us out when we are lost. You put us on your shoulders, delighted to bring us home. We thank you for your faithful love for us, which far exceeds anything we could ask or imagine. Please heal us from the lies we have believed that we are not valuable for ourselves, but only for our performance, looks, or what others can get from us. We ask you for the grace to experience your delight in us and that you always watch for us just as the prodigal son's father watched for him, and ran out to him "while he was still a long way off" (Luke 15:20). Thank you for the immensity of your tender love for me personally. Please give me the grace to accept this love ever more deeply. Amen.

Action Step

Recall an image from scripture that helps you see God's value for who you are (the creation account, the lost sheep, the lost coin, the prodigal son, etc.). Post a reminder of this somewhere you will encounter it throughout the day (on your phone, in your car, on the bathroom mirror, etc.). Allow this image to be a reminder that your value is inherent because of who God is and who he made you to be.

Journaling/Further Reflection

Ask God to help you identify any blocks within you that might prevent you from believing and experiencing the way God cherishes who you are. Ask him what he wants you to know about that and then note what he puts on your heart.

Scriptures for Meditation

Isaiah 43:4

Matthew 6:25-34

Luke 12:6-7

John 3:16

Romans 8:28

Titus 3:4-7

PRAYER

For me, prayer is a surge of the heart; it is a simple look turned toward Heaven, it is a cry of recognition and of love, embracing both trial and joy.

– St. Therese of Lisieux

Personal prayer is essential to internalizing the radical, profound intimacy the living God wants to experience with us. His love for us is infinite. It might be easy to read the last line and agree with it in our head, but in our heart still feel less than adequate, rejected, or forgotten. Our mind might be able to quickly categorize the statement as true, especially if we grew up in church, have studied Theology, or are religious or clergy. Yet, absorbing the Truth – God – is a lifelong process, one we will likely continue throughout eternity. It is not enough to know the description of God or how he desires to relate to us, even Satan knows the truth. We must make ourselves available to that relationship by spending time exposing our heart to him who exposes his heart to us.

There are many ways to pray, spontaneous intercession, praise and worship, the Rosary, litanies, or Mass. Contemplation is a quiet type of prayer in which we allow the Lord to permeate us at the core of who we are and transform us into him. To go to the source of water - a spring or a river - and draw water, but not consume it and allow our bodies to absorb the minerals and hydration would still leave us weak and dehydrated. St. John of the Cross talks about the importance of such prayer. He says,

> Learn to abide with attention in loving waiting upon God in a state of quiet. Contemplation is nothing else but a secret, peaceful, and loving infusion of God, which if admitted, will set the soul on fire with the spirit of love. [1]

Contemplation is spending time drinking in the living water of God's self-gift to us by being present to the Lord who is present to us. This is fundamentally being before him in quiet availability with our hearts open to his heart. He dwells within us through Baptism and we receive him in the Eucharist, but contemplation is the process of being infused with him.

Because contemplation is personal and intimate prayer, St. John says it is "secret." It is taking time away from other people, activities, and things, and being "in a state of quiet" paying attention to God and waiting on him. In that kind of waiting, we make time and space to let our hearts become available to be infused by his "spirit of love." This love sets our souls on fire. The caveat is that we must grant him permission to permeate us in order for this to happen. As we know and have seen in the connection figure, he is within us at our deepest core. We aren't trying to get him inside us from out there somewhere. Rather, we are allowing him to saturate us from the inside out.

Just like any relationship, growing closer and allowing someone into our heart and life is a process. The more we receive God, the more we love him in return, the more we feel safe with him, and the more we open ourselves up to him. In opening more, we permit him to more truly, fully, and deeply transform us and our lives. In relationships, we tend to reveal the good things about ourselves first. When the other person accepts us at that level, we have the courage to share some of our frailty with them and hide less of our weakness. Eventually, we feel confident enough in their good will toward us that we share with them our shame and pain. The same is true of how we grow in relationship with the Lord. This is why it takes time. It's not a limitation in him but in us, and one with which he is perfectly patient and persistent. He always calls us more deeply into his peace and love, and it requires vulnerability to respond to his invitation.

Shalom, the Hebrew word for peace, has a much richer meaning than we are used to. It doesn't simply mean the absence of conflict and stress. It is about wholeness, fulfillment, completion, and perfection. Jesus is the prince of peace. For this reason, it makes sense that spending time admitting him more deeply into every aspect of our lives draws us into deeper wholeness. It also draws us to holiness as we become more imbued with him. Thus, growing deeper in prayer can lead to us becoming more in touch with our brokenness or woundedness. This is an act of God's love and mercy because he desires to make us whole, but it requires courage on our part to allow him to do so.

Spending time in quiet certainly can seem to amplify the noise we may have inside us. Sometimes that noise is busy-ness. At other times, it may be that we are using internal noise to drown out pain. I remember a time in my life when even a moment of quiet was intolerable. I had to always have external sound turned up really loud to overcome the cacophony of chaos inside. I'd get in my car and immediately turn the music up and get home and instantly turn the television on. The expression 'peace and quiet' sounded crazy to me because quiet was anything but peaceful. As our own wounds are healed, the noise within ceases. We relate in less painful ways toward ourselves, and others. We put up fewer and fewer obstacles to the flow of God's love into us and through us to those he puts in our lives. The process and cycle of connection continues to deepen on all levels.

In order to succeed in the practice of contemplation it is helpful to make frequent use of the Sacrament of Reconciliation. Just as in any relationship, we are capable of participating with another even if there is something out of order between us, but it is much more intimate when the conflict is resolved. The same is true for our relationship with God. Resolving conflict by confessing our sins is the first step to repairing and building anew. Starting from a state of conflict will only start us off from a place of noise, rather than a place of quiet. In addition, when we practice contemplation with God it can be helpful to find something simple that can hold our attention on him. For some that may be a scripture or a title of Jesus. For others, it may be an image or statue of him that we picture in our mind or have present with us. The point here is not to busy our mind, but to open our heart to his love in a state of receptivity.

Questions for Reflection/Discussion

1. Do you find yourself avoiding being still and quiet with the Lord? Why or why not?
2. What is the internal noise you might be trying to drown?
3. Have you ever considered that prayer requires courage? What are your thoughts on this?
4. Have you found a key that opens the door to prayer for you? What is it? (Scripture, image, etc.)

Prayer

Lord, thank you for your infinite love for us and for desiring us to live in the fullness of that reality. Please grant us the grace to receive this truth more fully into the depths of our mind and heart, and be set ablaze by the fire of your love so our lives can give your warmth and light to all those we meet.

Action Step

Spend some time finding a scripture, quote, or picture that draws you into a sense of God's love.

Journaling/Further Reflection

If you have a sense of disquiet when you go to pray, ask the Lord to show you why that might be and ask him what he wants you to know about it.

Scriptures for Meditation

1 Kings 19:9-12

Psalm 37:7

Psalm 63:2-4

Matthew 6:5-8

John 7:37-44

2 Corinthians 4:18

GOD PROVIDES BOUNDARIES

Here, then, I have today set before you life and prosperity, death and doom. If you obey the commandments of the Lord, your God, which I enjoin on you today, loving him and walking in his ways, and keeping his commandments, statutes and decrees, you will live and grow numerous, and the Lord, your God, will bless you in the land you are entering to occupy. If, however, you turn away your hearts and will not listen, but are led astray and adore and serve other gods, I tell you now that you will certainly perish; you will not live a long life on the land which you are crossing the Jordan to enter and occupy.

– Deuteronomy 30:15-18

The reason we started with the concept of connection to God was so we could have a clear understanding of the fact he is with us, knows us intimately, values us for who we are, and sent his Son to save us by emptying himself on the Cross. He is continually emptying himself in the Eucharist and pouring his graces and mercy upon us, which draw us into the life of the Trinity. He makes his home in us through baptism and animates us by his Spirit. We cannot let go of this foundation as we consider this section on boundaries. If we do, we risk having a very distorted image of God.

As the author of life and our creator, he knows what limits are good for us, foster our health, and lead us to deepest intimacy with him, our fulfillment and our prince of peace. The same way he set limits for the ocean, knowing what is good and necessary to foster life, so does he do for us. There is something very different, though, about his boundaries for us. He has given us free will, which means we can choose to embrace him and be embraced by him. We can run to our Father's loving and protective arms or we can refuse them and their protection for us.

Our free will allows us to choose whether to abide by his law. We may choose to see his law as a set of rules that he requires us to follow, but the danger in this is it can very quickly lead to bitterness, judgment, and resentment. This was the mindset of the older brother in the story of the prodigal son who could not tolerate the father's mercy. The father's goodness caused him outrage, which revealed his own lack of connection to his father. He was obeying the rules as boxes to check off and a way of keeping his nose clean. This clearly did not lead to a depth of intimate relationship and certainly prevented him from being a conduit of grace to his brother. It's difficult to imagine the older brother had much satisfaction in life beyond his self-righteousness.

There are times I have to refuse to give my dog things because I know they would not be good for her. Her limitations of language and understanding prevent me from being able to explain to her why I can't let her go off-leash near traffic or why I can't let her eat food that would be unhealthy for her. Sometimes, it hurts to say no to her and I have to remind myself it is for her own good. Indulging her desires, knowing they would be dangerous or deadly for her, would actually be an act of selfishness, not of love for her. How much greater the chasm between God's understanding and ours! How much more does the Father know about what is good for us! His law is consistent because his wisdom is perfect and his loving protection is unwavering. Of course, we can choose to see God's boundaries as requirements, because they do require our free response. The much fuller truth is that his law is first and foremost a providential and protective gift. We can respond with grudge or gratitude.

Blessed Julian of Norwich, a 14th century mystic, was gifted with revelations from our Lord himself. From what was shown to her she wrote *Revelations of Divine Love* in which she shares a profoundly compassionate and merciful thought, "God sees sin as pain in us."[1] He knows partaking of forbidden fruit makes us sick and it excites compassion from his heart. When we wander off he seeks us out and waits to embrace us when we turn back to him. He has already prepared for our return home to him by the mercy he offers us and which he longs for us to experience. He bathes our wounds, even those of our own making. He's just that good.

Questions for Reflection and Discussion

1. Do you experience the sacrament of reconciliation as a time of fear and shame, or as a time of intimate reunion with God?
2. Why do you think you experience the sacrament of confession the way you do?
3. What strikes you as the greatest difference in seeing God's boundaries as for us versus something that he wants from us?

4. Does considering that God's limits are an expression of his love change how you see his law and/or how you see him?

Prayer

"Oh, the depth of the riches of the wisdom and knowledge of God! How inscrutable are his judgments and how unsearchable his ways! 'For who has known the mind of the Lord or who has been his counselor?' 'Or who has given him anything that he may be repaid should?' For from him and through him and for him are all things. To him be glory forever! Amen."

- Romans 11:33-36

All good and loving Father, your protective arms reach out to embrace us and keep us safely on the path to eternal joy with you. Thank you for your infinite mercy for the times we've chosen our understanding over your boundless wisdom and goodness. Please give us the grace to follow Jesus, the way to you. In his holy name we pray. Amen.

Action Step

If there are any aspects of morality with which you struggle, ask the Lord to show you how it is an expression of his loving protection for you.

Journaling/Further Reflection

Do you most often experience God's law as gift or as demand? Consider if this might be based on your past experiences of limits from parents or early caregivers. Ask the Lord what he wants you to know.

Scriptures for Meditation

Deuteronomy 28:1

Deuteronomy 30:19

Joshua 1:8

Psalm 119: 165

Jeremiah 29:11

Ephesians 2:4-9

GOD'S OPENNESS

Behold this heart which has so loved men as to spare Itself nothing, even to exhausting and consuming Itself, to testify to them Its love…

– Jesus to St. Margaret Mary Alacoque

The God of the entire universe who is all-knowing and all-powerful is open in relating to us. One of my favorite scripture verses is from the short little book, Baruch, "Blessed are we, O Israel; for what pleases God is known to us!" (Baruch 4:4). How amazing it is that he chooses to make himself known to us! Not only does he reveal who he is, but also what pleases him. There is tenderness in his self-revelation and, given our free will, vulnerability. What if we didn't know how to please him who loves us so personally and intimately? How we'd long to know how to bridge that distance!

Throughout time, we see God stooping further and further to show himself to us. Knowing we would many times reject him, he still so desires relationship with us that he became incarnate. In doing so, he manifested who he is to us in a manner to which we could relate. Of all the ways he could have done so, he came as a tiny, helpless baby and has made himself even more vulnerable - to the point of a gruesome crucifixion and death. Finally, he remains in the Eucharist where he hides his majesty in bread and wine. In the late 1600s, Jesus revealed his sacred heart to St. Margaret Mary Alacoque. He asked her to remind us how much he loves all mankind and how he longs for our love.

It's important for us to take note of the Lord's openness with us. He starts from a place of seeing each of us as his dear children who are very good, he treasures us beyond measure, promises to provide for and protect us, and to work all things for our good (Romans 8:28). He gives us the freedom to choose or refuse him, and then intimately bares his heart to us. He wants an intimate relationship with us, but only one of our free choosing. He is omnipotent, but doesn't force himself on us. The Lord who can easily go through locked doors chooses to stand at the door of our hearts and knock (Revelation 3:20).

When someone knocks at our door, we can ignore it, dismiss the person, speak to them through the closed door, open it and talk to them on the porch, welcome them in as a guest, or bring them in to live with us in deep communion. What is our response to the Lord? He has knocked and continues to knock daily. It is up to us to answer.

Questions for Reflection and Discussion

1. What comes to mind when you think about God's openness with you?
2. Is there anything about his vulnerability that surprises you? If so, what?
3. Is there a particular memory, thought, or emotion that comes to mind in considering Jesus opening himself to you?

Prayer

Most high God, omnipotent Lord of the universe, we give you thanks and praise for revealing yourself to us in the expanse and beauty of creation. Thank you for making yourself known to us in an infinite number of ways. More than all this, we are humbled and in awe of how you empty yourself for us and open yourself to us longing for our love. Please give us eyes to see you and ears to hear you knocking at the door of our heart, in Jesus' name. Amen.

Action Step

Spend a few minutes each day with the concept or an image of the Lord opening himself to you. Thank him and ask for the grace to let him in more deeply.

Journaling/Further Reflection

Consider the Lord opening himself totally to you. What is moved in your heart when you think of this? Wonder? Delight? Fear? Confusion? Tell the Lord and ask him what he wants you to know.

Scriptures for Meditation

Isaiah 53:7

Zechariah 9:9

Luke 2:4-7

John 6:54-57

John 19:31-37

2 Corinthians 8:9

OPENNESS WITH GOD

If you knew the gift of God and who is saying to you,

'Give me a drink,' you would have asked

him and he would have given you living water.

– John 4:10

The human body is made up of about seventy percent water. Water is necessary for healthy energy levels, flushing toxins and plays a key role in the proper functioning of our whole system. We need it for refreshment on a hot day, for cleansing of dirt and sweat, and it is essential to our lives and the lives of the plants and animals we consume for nutrition. Water is crucial. When a water source is stagnant, we know to be suspicious of it because it can more likely be a breeding ground for bacteria and parasites.

Jesus doesn't just tell us he will give us water, or that he will give us flowing water. He says he will give us living water! This water is his very life! His only requirement is that we be open by acknowledging our need to him. To ask him is the only thing the woman at the well had to do (John 4:4-30) and all we have to do, too.

For some of us, it's difficult to express our needs, even to Jesus, because we experienced pain when we were vulnerable in the past. If others have used our vulnerability against us, it can make us feel weak and unwilling to admit our need. Perhaps we've asked the Lord in, but we keep him sequestered to the foyer of our hearts and make other rooms off limits to him. Maybe there is a particularly messy room we think we haven't sufficiently tidied and are ashamed to let him into, or a room we are too scared to enter at all. Jesus honors our desire for control of our own inner self, and knows we need to pace ourselves. When we allow Jesus to bring his living water to us, even if it is only to the foyer, he can begin to heal our wounds, calm our fears, remove our shame, and establish his spring of living water in the depths of our being.

Our need for this living, flowing water is as essential to our souls as clean water is to our bodies. Jesus constantly and eternally supplies us with this heavenly water. We only need to remember it is there and draw from him. Living water would, of course, be flowing. Let's not stop the flow with sandbags and dams of sin and pain, but allow Jesus free reign to flow into every area of our minds and hearts, and through us to others.

Wherever we are on our journey, however long we've been walking with the Lord, there is more to open to him because he has so much more of himself for us. We are known intimately, treasured unconditionally, and he is solicitous to protect us. He makes himself vulnerable and accessible to us at every moment, every day and night. All we need to do is to open up and ask for more of him.

Questions for Reflection and Discussion

1. In what ways and at what times do you experience the greatest ability to be open to the Lord?
2. What areas are the most difficult to open to him? Why?
3. In what areas would you like to experience greater openness with him? Tell him.

Prayer

Come, Holy Spirit, fill the hearts of your faithful and enkindle in them the fire of your love.

V. Send forth your Spirit and they shall be created.

R. And you shall renew the face of the earth.

Let us pray.

O God, who by the light of the Holy Spirit,

did instruct the hearts of the faithful,

grant us in the same Spirit to be truly wise

and ever to rejoice in his consolation,

through Christ our Lord.

Amen.[1]

Action Step

Ask the Lord to show you if there are areas of your life and your heart you have not yet opened to him or which he desires to fill even more fully with his living water and then give him permission to give you his life in these areas.

Journaling/Further Reflection

When Jesus met the Samaritan woman at the well, it was noon, the hottest part of the day and the time people were least likely to draw water – she was hiding. She was hiding because of her shame, but he longed to bring his light to her areas of darkness so she might live in freedom. Ask the Lord to show you if you hide in any way because of shame. Spend some time writing to the Lord inviting him into these areas. Take time to receive him into those rooms.

Scriptures for Meditation

Job 13:15

Psalm 119:18

Matthew 16:24

Luke 24:45

Romans 12:2

James 4:7

Revelation 3:20

KNOWING GOD

For I am convinced that neither death, nor life, nor angels, nor principalities, nor present things, nor future things, nor powers, nor height, nor depth, nor any other creature, will be able to separate us from the love of God in Christ Jesus our Lord.

– Romans 8:38-39.

Knowing God is crucial. We've already been discussing connection to God and mostly it's been about who he is and how he is toward us. We see he is personal, knows us perfectly, desires for us to experience profound intimacy with him, cherishes us beyond measure, and operates in our best interest, (which is far better than we could ever hope for or imagine). He protects us and provides for us always and perfectly in the ways necessary to draw us to him. When we stay within his loving boundaries, we remain in him and under the shelter of his wings. If we move out from under his protection by sin, he immediately takes us back, time and again, when we turn back to him in repentance.

We can miss all this. We can believe God wants something from us that we really can't give him. We can live our lives with the burden of assuming he is harsh and demanding and his love must be earned. If we wear the lenses through which we perceive him as distant, we will interpret events as though he is cold and uncaring. There are all sorts of different versions of imperfect lenses, but only the ones of truth help us see him clearly and experience him accurately.

If someone close to us is misunderstood, we might be surprised or maybe even a little defensive of them. That's because we know them, who they are and their heart, and we readily come to an accurate understanding of their behavior in a given circumstance. We have to begin with an understanding of God as all good and all loving when we consider the circumstances and events of our lives or we'll misunderstand who he is. If we don't start there, we will never be able to understand what he does or allows to happen. We can't interpret him through the lens of our limited understanding of circumstances, but rather we need to remain trusting of who he has revealed himself to be when times are difficult.

Inevitably, life has times of trial and challenge. Sadly, we can be so fearful of displeasing God we can sometimes rush to a conclusion without starting from a right understanding of who he is. We can feel so lonely, isolated, and forgotten. We might put inordinate pressure on ourselves to earn his love, when the truth is he is madly in love with us. Our lenses, like the lenses of a pair of binoculars, can be adjusted. As we grow closer to him, the focus continues to become clearer. He is infinitely loving and good, so there is always room for greater clarity in our vision of him. This clarity is gained as it is in all relationships, by spending time together in open communication. It is not enough to know about him. We must seek to know him and to open up to him in return. This relationship requires us to reciprocate.

Questions for Reflection and Discussion

1. When you find yourself struggling in life, through what lenses are you usually viewing God? (e.g., aloof, demanding, etc.)

2. Why might you see him that way?

3. What aspect of God's goodness is the most difficult for you to internalize? Why?

Prayer

Watch Cory Asbury's video for his song "Reckless Love"[1] at the following link: https://www.youtube.com/watch?v=Sc6SSHuZvQE

Action Step

Write yourself a note or letter about who God truly is that you can read when you are in difficult times.

Journaling/Further Reflection

Take some time to reflect on your note or letter from the Action Step and ask the Lord to reveal to you what he particularly wants you to take to heart.

Scriptures for Meditation

Psalm 46:10

Psalm 119:10

Jeremiah 9:23-24

John 17:3

2 Peter 3:18

VALUING GOD

Jesu, joy of man's desiring,

Holy wisdom, love most bright;

Drawn by Thee, our souls aspiring

Soar to uncreated light.

– lyrics attributed to Robert Bridges

In taking up this section on valuing God, something a friend of mine once said to me comes to mind, "God can't be a priority." Her point was that he is all; he is the only priority. Consider the passion of our Lord: if Jesus' commitment to us wasn't absolute, things could have turned out radically different. He could have abandoned the cross at any point. However, because he is consumed with love for us, there was nothing to evaluate or reconsider. He didn't need to do a cost/benefit analysis as to whether we would respond well to the love he would show to us and the graces he would merit for us.

Do we value the Lord the same way? If we don't start from a firm understanding that he knows us and has the big picture of this life, and the next, perfectly in view, then we are likely to have a honey-do list for the Lord. If we don't realize the depth of his consuming passion for us personally, then we're likely to default into relating to him out of servile fear. Without realizing that the limits he sets for us are a manifestation of his protection for us, we'll treat him like a vending machine, dispensing the grace we need to accomplish our plans, since we presume we have to look out for ourselves. We'll be insulted, angry, and feel rejected and abandoned when his way is not our way.

When we relate to the Lord by valuing him for who he is, not what he does or what he can do for us, we're able to remain consistent. Though we may struggle with painful emotions at times, our regard doesn't ebb and flow based on how we evaluate his performance. It's a stance of submission to his wisdom, but primarily an acceptance of his infinite passion.

Let's not cheat ourselves out of the greatest romance the world has ever known and the greatest lover for whom we could ever long by focusing on the 'how'. When we keep our focus on the 'why' of letting the all-loving God love us and loving him in return, the details don't take care of themselves, they are taken care of by him according to his infinite wisdom and in a way that will, one day, blow our minds.

Questions for Reflection and Discussion

1. Do you tend to relate to God with a focus on what you want him to do? What is it you find yourself wanting from him?
2. Do you consider he has more for you than your limited understanding can figure out or ask? Why or why not?
3. Do you find it difficult to trust his love for you? Why or why not?

Prayer

Most high and glorious God, lover of our soul, we thank you for who you are and that you are trustworthy. Please help us to receive your love so completely, that we may lose ourselves and thereby find ourselves in your heart. We ask all this in Jesus' name. Amen.

Action Step

Consider making the intentions of Jesus' Sacred Heart your only intention for this week and consider what his intentions might be.

Journaling/Further Reflection

Ask the Lord to show you if there are any areas of your life where you don't believe his design and power are capable of accomplishing anything greater than your own hopes. Ask him to show you why this is difficult for you to trust him with and what he wants you to know about it.

Scriptures for Meditation

1 Chronicles 16:34

Psalm 63:1

Psalm 71:8

Psalm 1:6

Habakkuk 3:17-18

John 4:24

EMBRACING GOD'S BOUNDARIES

For I know the plans I have in mind for you, says the Lord, plans for your welfare, not for woe! plans to give you a future full of hope.

– Jeremiah 29:11

In our connection to God and fully seeking to respond to his love for us, we now come to the concept of embracing the boundaries he sets for us. We've discussed morality as God's protection over us, since he is our all-loving creator. The Ten Commandments are the starting point of these boundaries. They lay out for us, in the most foundational way, how to live under the umbrella of God's protection. He's not lying in wait for us to break his law so he can zap us. Rather, as the good shepherd, he provides safe pasture knowing what we need and what truly nourishes us.

And so, we move from the Ten Commandments to the Beatitudes. It would have been too much for these teachings to have come in any other way than by the mouth of Jesus who made them incarnate for us. He has called us to follow in his footsteps, not just to obey the rules but also to be one with him. He whom we are called to espouse forever in Heaven is our crucified love. In the Gospel of John, Jesus told us:

> If the world hates you, realize that it hated me first. If you belonged to the world, the world would love its own; but because you do not belong to the world, and I have chosen you out of the world, the world hates you. Remember the word I spoke to you, 'No slave is greater than his master.' If they persecuted me, they will also persecute you" (John 15: 18 – 20).

Obedience to the law will be empty and confounding, but taking up our crosses and following him will lead to deepest intimacy. Rules for the sake of rules leads to turning inward. Receiving the boundaries he sets for us as coming from the heart of our all-loving Father, rather than from a place of control, leads to boundless life and gratitude.

As a therapist, I have seen others longing or even adamantly determined to obtain an end they cannot see would be disastrous. It's been humbling because I know the Lord has seen me do the same. At times he's said no to my petitions and I've taken it as rejection, proof of a lack of love, when in truth it is quite the opposite. Not only that, but he'd rather risk being misunderstood by me than to give me anything other than what is the absolute best for me.

Our Lady of Lourdes told Saint Bernadette Soubirous, "I do not promise you happiness in this world, but in the next."[1] We know the Lord has our eternal good in mind for us. Whatever limits he sets or requires of us in this life, or whatever he might ask us to endure is to our ultimate and perpetual good. In her book, *Crucified Love*, Ilia Delio writes of God's goodness, "This nature of the good underscores a Trinity of eternal love whose immensity of divine goodness is such that no greater good can be thought."[2] Put simply, if we think something is desirable or a good idea, it is only a shadow of the goodness of God.

Questions for Reflection and Discussion

1. Have you ever taken care of children or a pet and experienced the child or animal seemingly regarding your protection as meanness? Describe the experience from your

perspective as the caregiver and consider God acting in this way toward you.

2. What might be preventing you from seeing that God's limits for you are in fact his protection?
3. Do you tend to see God's law as what he wants from you or what he has for you?
4. If you look at God's law as what he wants for you, why do you think that is?

Prayer

"Most high, glorious God, enlighten the darkness of my heart and give me, Lord, a correct faith, a certain hope, a perfect charity, sense and knowledge, so that I may carry out your holy and true command."[3] – St. Francis of Assisi

Action Step

Consider your life. In what area do you tend to feel God is asking the most from you? Ask him to show you what he has for you in that same area.

Journaling/Further Reflection

Spend some time considering the paradox of a personal cross as a mysterious gift and note what comes to you here.

Scriptures for Meditation

Proverbs 3:5-6

Psalm 16:11

Psalm 119:105

Luke 9:23

1 Thessalonians 5:18

Hebrews 10:36

SUFFERING

He was spurned and avoided by men, a man of suffering, accustomed to infirmity, one of those from whom men hide their faces, spurned, and we held him in no esteem.

– Isaiah 53:3

There are times in all our lives when we go through trials: illness, rejection, abuse, death of a loved one, or loss of a dream, just to name a few. When such things happen, it can be difficult to stay rooted in the truth of God's connection to us. Even if we've had mountaintop experiences of God's love, sufferings such as these can cause us to feel isolated, disconnected, or abandoned, even from our all-loving creator.

Let's take a look at the example of the Blessed Virgin Mary when the archangel Gabriel appeared to her. He greeted her as "favored one" (Luke 1:28). He went on to promise that the son she would conceive would rule with greatness over an everlasting kingdom. Yet, she is the Mother of Sorrows. She went on to be told, by Simeon, that a sword of sorrow would pierce her heart. She had to flee to Egypt to protect her newborn baby, watched him be contradicted continually throughout his life, deserted by his closest friends, mocked and mercilessly tortured, and subjected to a shameful death without seeing the fulfillment of those promises. It was not because God didn't see who she was or value her. Remember, she is highly favored. We see the greatest example in Jesus himself, whom the Father called his beloved Son, and yet the cup of abuse and death was not taken away from him.

These cases show us that God has a much bigger big picture than ours. He is outside of time and sees all eternity. When suffering comes, it is not a result of not being loved and valued by the Lord. He will work all things to our good, even if it does not happen in this life. We're used to watching sports or playing games - whoever has the most points at the end is victorious. In this life, we don't see the scoreboard. Only after death will we know fully how God, who will not be outdone in generosity, will repay all we have to endure.

When Jesus was betrayed, Peter was so terrified of physical suffering he three times denied knowing him. Even so, only days after the Lord's resurrection the Acts of the Apostles presents us with a bold and courageous Peter proclaiming the truth regardless of threat and persecution. He even rejoiced when he was physically abused for the sake of preaching about Jesus. Peter finally learned through the Lord's resurrection what Jesus had told him all along; His kingdom is not of this world. When we remember the same fact, we are able to keep our view on eternity rather than seeking our reward in this life.

Questions for Reflection and Discussion

1. Recall a time of suffering or trial in your life. Did you question God's love, value, or protection of you? Why or why not?
2. What, if anything, have you found helpful to remind yourself of God's love and to connect to him during painful times?

Prayer

Lord Jesus, we know you suffered and left us an example of faith in our Father's love. Please grant us the grace to follow you. Remind us of the Father's constant love for us, even in the most difficult times. In your holy name we pray. Amen.

Action Step

Consider what it is you are most caused to doubt about God during times of suffering. Write a letter to yourself reminding yourself of God's love that you can read when difficulties come your way.

Journaling/Further Reflection

Consider your answer from number two in the discussion questions. Ask the Lord what he wants you to know about that and note what he brings to mind.

Scriptures for Meditation

Sirach 2

Wisdom 3:1-9

Luke 2:34-35

Romans 11:33-36

Hebrews 4:14-16

POWERLESSNESS

Have among yourselves the same attitude that is also yours in Christ Jesus, who though he was in the form of God, did not regard equality with God something to be grasped. Rather, he emptied himself, taking the form of a slave, coming in human likeness; and found human in appearance, he humbled himself, becoming obedient to death, even death on a cross.

- Philippians 2:5-7

The common denominator throughout almost every experience that causes us suffering is that of powerlessness. As people, we have limited ability to affect change in situations that are difficult for us or for those we care about. This in no way diminishes our fundamental value; it simply part of the human condition. We come into the world almost totally powerless. As we grow and develop and gain power, we have to learn to navigate our abilities without running over others, literally and metaphorically. Even though our ability to cause change increases as time goes by, we still have limitations. These limitations can at times mean inconvenience for us and at other times they may lead to great suffering. Regardless of our age, we always have a limit to our power.

What we do with our powerlessness greatly affects our spiritual life, peace, and joy. If we meet times when we don't have power with pride, our self-reliant response will fail. Our failure leads to shame and shame leads to a desire to hide. When we hide, the isolation can lead to disconnection and deeper suffering. We don't have to look very far to see this pattern in people of all ages when faced with challenging situations. There is a better response. We can choose to accept the fact of our helplessness and meet the difficulty with gratitude that all will be used by God as gift for us, no matter how painful it may seem at the time. When we choose this way of interpreting a difficult situation, our faith and hope in God transforms the very same situation. Even though from the outside it may seem that nothing has changed, our ability to stay aware of the truth that God is with us and for us can help us to remain at peace.

St. Francis of Assisi had a particular devotion to Jesus' incarnation, his suffering and death on the cross, and the Eucharist.

He was awestruck by the humility of the omnipotent God who chose to make himself powerless to stoop down to us and raise us up to him. In doing so, Jesus gave us these three profound examples of how to embrace our own powerlessness. When we have times when we are painfully out of control, we can take consolation in the fact that the Lord understands our experience and we can trust that he is present to us through them. They can be occasions for intimacy with him if we choose to endure them with him. There is something about accepting and even embracing our powerlessness that prevents us from complicating already difficult situations. Walking through the trouble with Jesus enables us to reject the temptation to put inordinate pressure on ourselves (or others) to fix things that are beyond our control. Once we've done all the Lord has asked of us, we lay the experience at his feet with hope, not for a particular outcome, but hope in him and his goodness that will use the trial for our good.

Questions for Reflection and Discussion

1. What emotions arise in you when you think of Jesus choosing to embrace powerlessness as a baby, at his death, and in the Eucharist?

2. What emotions arise in you when you think of being powerless?
3. What do you think about the idea of embracing your powerlessness as imitation of the Lord?
4. Do you think it would affect your experiences of suffering to consider them as occasions for intimacy with the Lord, as a sharing in his powerlessness and an imitation of him?

Prayer

Lord Jesus, we thank you for the immensity of your omnipotence and the exceeding humility with which you laid your majesty aside for our sake, to embrace the incarnation, your suffering, and to remain with us in the Holy Eucharist. Thank you for showing us how deeply you desire intimacy with us and for leaving us examples of how to embrace the powerlessness of our humanity. Help us to remember that you are with us always in the Blessed Sacrament. We pray all this in your holy name. Amen.

Action Step

Find a time our Lord set aside his omnipotence for our sake and place a reminder of it, either as a scripture quote, an image, a song, etc., somewhere you will see it throughout the week.

Journaling/Reflection

Ask the Lord to show you what you most fear about your own powerlessness and invite his perfect love into that place of fear.

Scriptures for Meditation

Mark 10:45

Luke 1:26-38

John 13:3-72

Corinthians 8:9

Philippians 2:5-11

Hebrews 4:15

GOING DEEPER

My deepest me is God.

– St. Catherine of Genoa

When we take a moment to look at nature, we find that life is always a process. Whether it is the acorn becoming a mighty oak, an egg hatching into a duckling, or a baby growing into an adult, life is a process. Since physical life is a process, why would emotional and spiritual life be any different? We would never look at a toddler and think they are wrong or bad for not being an adult. The very idea is outrageous, and would deny the beauty of the child and the process God has made.

The process of growth surrounds us. It is beautiful and wonderful to know that we always have more room for development in our relationship with God, as formation is a lifelong process! He is infinite! We grow when we allow him to increase our capacity for him and receive more of who he is. The more we receive of him, the more we are transformed into who we really are, the more our capacity for him increases, and so on.

Like any relationship, we first approach another by opening up and revealing the good things about ourselves. Next, we might show some of our less glorious moments, and begin to be vulnerable. Finally, we reveal our pain, our shame, and our weakness, that which we hold deep within us, hidden from view until we know it's safe. Once we have a firm trust in another person's acceptance of us, a bond is developed. We find this same pattern as we grow closer to the Lord.

As we begin to improve our relationship with our creator, we begin to see things as if through God's eyes, which allows us to see Him more clearly and to be drawn more deeply into union with Him. This doesn't happen once and is complete. Instead, we tend to follow a winding staircase as our deepening union with God reveals to us more dross, which we are then able to release. Liberation from our own garbage helps us know God even more closely and become more one with him. Good mental and physical health work together with our growing spiritual health. They are not at odds with each other, but together bring us into a state of wholeness and holiness that is our birthright as sons and daughters of God.

St. Thomas Aquinas said, "Grace does not destroy nature, but perfects it."[1] We need personal integration and rightly ordered relationships. By seeking God's kingdom first, everything else falls into place. As we learn with the help of God to quiet the clamor and chaos of disorder, his grace brings wholeness to our lives. God's perfecting work leads to fulfillment and order, personally and interpersonally

Questions for Reflection and Discussion

1. In what ways can you see you have grown in your relationship with God over time?
2. What areas of your own formation are you growing in the most at this time?
3. How might it help to consider your relationship with God as a process?
4. How might it help you to consider other people's relationships with God as a process?

Prayer

Lord Jesus, we thank you for coming to us to reveal the heart of the Father and to redeem us in your love. It was not enough for you to save all mankind, but you desire a personal relationship with us. We want to grow closer to you every day. Please give us the grace to do so and to be patient with ourselves in the process. In your holy name we pray. Amen.

Action Step

What's one thing you can do to take a step closer in the way you relate to the Lord? Take that step this week.

Journaling/Further Reflection

Ask the Lord to show you what the biggest block is to your receiving and responding to more of his love at this time in your life. Ask him what he wants you to know about that and journal what comes to you.

Scriptures for Meditation

Jeremiah 29:13

Luke 2:52

James 4:8

1 Peter 2:2

CONNECTION TO SELF

One of the scribes, when he came forward and heard them disputing and saw how well he had answered them, asked him, "Which is the first of all the commandments?" Jesus replied, "The first is this: 'Hear, O Israel! The Lord our God is Lord is alone! You shall love the Lord your God with all your heart, with all your soul, with all your mind, and with all your strength. 'The second is this: You shall love your neighbor as yourself. 'There is no commandment greater than these.

– Mark 12: 28-31

Healthy confidence and self-worth are fruits of personal integration. The same factors that are essential for connection to God are also essential for connection to self – being known, valued, and open, and having healthy boundaries. Ideally, a child experiences being known, valued, accepted, and protected by good and loving parents. When this happens, it's a natural bridge to having self-knowledge and self-acceptance.

So, why is it important to talk about this? Did we just move from talking about spirituality in the previous section to selfishness and being self-consumed? Not at all! Take a look again at the scripture from Mark 12 at the beginning of this section. The teacher who approached Jesus asked him which law is the most important. Jesus answered his question by also telling him the second most important law: To love our neighbor as we love ourselves. This answer hinges love of neighbor on love of self, revealing that in order to have the former, we must also have the latter.

As we consider loving ourselves, let's remember what true love looks like. 1 Corinthians 13:4-8, a passage we might already be familiar with, details the definition of love:

> Love is patient, love is kind. It is not jealous, is not pompous, it is not inflated, it is not rude, it does not seek its own interests, it is not quick-tempered, it does not brood over injury, it does not rejoice over wrongdoing but rejoices with the truth. It bears all things, believes all things, hopes all things, endures all things. Love never fails.

You might be thinking, "That sounds great, but where am I supposed to get all this love to give to others?" The truth is, God who is love dwells within us. First, we must believe it – more and more. Then we can begin to receive it and embrace it, and allow his love to modify our own ways of thinking and flow out from us toward others. Being more deeply formed in God's mind causes us to continually reform our ways of thinking and behaving until we are eventually thoroughly transformed. That's holiness, which is the goal of this life for all of us. It's not just for clergy and religious. We are all called to be holy.

If we pour a large amount of water into a container, the container will soon begin to overflow, much like we are called to overflow with God's love for each other. Even if Niagara Falls is poured into a colander, at the end we will still have an empty colander. When we tear ourselves down in our own thoughts or self-talk, we poke colander-like holes in our hearts. No wonder we feel so empty! When our relationship with our own self is in shambles from our constant criticism, all the helps God wants to give us can't find a place to hold on. Even forming and maintaining a healthy external relationship becomes nearly impossible when our internal relationship is hurtful. Next thing we know, we hit a rough patch in an external relationship and we begin to wonder where God is in it all.

St. Thomas Aquinas said, "What is received is received according to the mode of the receiver."[1] The way we relate to ourselves can be considered our mode. If we don't believe we are lovable, we won't be able to believe someone else loves us and their love can't reach us. For this reason, it is crucial that we make an act of our will and conscious efforts to open to God's grace so that when he tells us he loves us, we can allow his grace to convince our hearts that it is true. Then we will receive what we can and regard ourselves a little more charitably. He will tell us again, and we will embrace the truth a bit more, and so on. It's a never-ending cycle; since there's always more of him and we, with our cracks, tend to be a bit leaky.

It's essential for us to make a shift in how we choose to relate to ourselves - it is a necessary part of being spiritually and emotionally responsible. Otherwise we are very prone to make the mistake of making God responsible for our emotions when we are the ones making ourselves miserable. If we constantly send ourselves the message that we're not lovable, it only stands to reason it will be hard for us to believe he or anyone else could or would love me. Taking on the mind of Christ includes shifting how we think of ourselves to how he regards us. That is absolutely non-negotiable if we really believe he is God.

In the upcoming sections, we'll break down the same aspects of connection we considered in connection to the Lord – knowing, valuing, and having healthy boundaries – so we can grow in our ability to fully accept, receive, and embody Jesus' words and redeeming love for us.

Questions for Reflection and Discussion

1. Have you ever considered the idea of being connected to yourself?
2. Think of people you've known who have seemed truly loving. Do you think they love themselves, too?
3. Is it surprising to you that the Lord includes you loving yourself with the most important laws?
4. Is there anything you might do differently if you treated yourself more lovingly?

Prayer

Heavenly Father, we thank you that you call us your children and that you ask us to treat ourselves as such. Please give us the grace to see ourselves with your loving eyes and extol the greatness of your mercy and fidelity. You are our good Father, and we long to be conformed to you in all ways, even in imitating your tender and powerful love for us. In Jesus' name we pray. Amen.

Action Step

Consider one way you treat yourself, in thought or deed, which you do not consider loving. In place of that behavior, relate to yourself the way our Lord does.

Journaling/Further Reflection

Ask the Lord to show you any areas in which you tend to be less than loving (see 1 Corinthians 13) toward yourself. Ask the Holy Spirit to show you why these are areas of struggle and how he sees you. Record your thoughts.

Scriptures for Meditation

Proverbs 4:23

Psalm 139:14

Matthew 22:37-39

Mark 12:31

1 John 4:19

KNOWING MYSELF

...for what a man is before God, that he is and nothing more.

– St. Francis of Assisi

What is the truth of who we are as God sees us? In creating us he made us in his own image and likeness and called us very good. (Genesis 1:31) He called us his own and bound himself in covenant to us. He has a plan for our good. He sent his only Son to reveal the depths of his love and mercy to us and to adopt us as his children. He has every hair of our head counted. (Luke 12:7) He gives himself to us intimately through the Eucharist and runs to embrace us as soon as we turn to make our way back to him after we fall.

In being a missionary of God's love to ourselves, it's necessary to know something about ourselves. It's important to take time to get to know what we need in order to be at our best. When we grow in knowledge of our strengths and weaknesses and learn what motivates us, we are able to understand ourselves as the gift

God made. This self-knowledge gives us an insight into the needs of others, as well. Coming to understand ourselves better doesn't mean that we will necessarily look to the fulfillment of our selfish desires; rather we are more equipped to stay along the narrow way to the Lord. It really is like taking a step back and considering our soul as a little child. With greater understanding of who we are as individuals, we can have better patience, wisdom, and counsel for ourselves. This is self-talk at its best.

Without true self-knowledge, we inevitably end up desperate to be known by others. While we are made for community with our brothers and sisters, it is meant to be from a place of health, reciprocity and freedom, not a place of anxious need. Sadly, if we are frantic to be known by others, we devalue ourselves, disregard the healthy boundaries we need, risk crossing others' limits, and end up relating to them as a means to an end, without being present to the gift they are. Happily, when we start from a place of being filled by the Lord's knowledge of us and taking on his mindset about ourselves, we start from a place of fullness rather than starvation. This is how we can foster peace in our lives and in our relationships and drastically reduce unnecessary complications, pain and even trauma.

Using how God sees us as the gold standard of truth makes us fearless in self-examination. It's amazing how powerful this can be - like an inoculation against comparison, judgment and rejection, even of ourselves. A quote I mentioned before is "God sees sin as pain in us"[1] from Blessed Julian of Norwich. When we look at ourselves with God's eyes, we don't hide in shame and can get back on the right track much more quickly when we stumble. Even our sin, as God sees it, is an occasion for compassion. We don't have to worry that forgiving ourselves for sin or weakness will lead to complacency if we remain open to the Lord. The compassion of God is always oriented to making us more like him.

Questions for Reflection and Discussion

1. What are some places or times you feel closest to God?
2. When you feel closest to God, do you see yourself the way you believe he sees you during those times? Why or why not?
3. What situations in your life do you find most challenging?

4. What is a strength you have for which you are grateful to God?

Prayer

In praying this song, "Be Still My Soul," speak to yourself with patient reassurance, reminding yourself of God's goodness and power. This is a great example of how you can gently guide yourself and minister His love to yourself.

Be Still My Soul

Be still, my soul: the Lord is on thy side;

bear patiently the cross of grief or pain;

leave to thy God to order and provide;

in ev'ry change He faithful will remain.

Be still, my soul: thy best, thy heav'nly Friend

thro' thorny ways leads to a joyful end.

Be still, my soul: when dearest friends depart,

and all is darkened in the vale of tears,

then shalt thou better know His love, His heart,

who comes to soothe thy sorrow and thy fears.

Be still, my soul: the waves and winds still know

His voice, who ruled them while He dwelt below.

Be still, my soul: the hour is hast'ning on

when we shall be forever with the Lord,

when disappointment, grief, and fear are gone,

sorrow forgot, love's purest joys restored.

Be still, my soul: when change and tears are past,

all safe and blessed we shall meet at last.[2]

– lyrics by Katharina VonSchlegel

Action Step

Find a picture you like of yourself as a baby or very small child. Take a picture of it and save it as your wallpaper and lock screen on your phone or post it somewhere you'll see it frequently for the next month. You may want to put it in a prayer book you use frequently so you encounter it when you're actively available to God's presence. Notice if this helps you grow in having greater compassion for yourself.

Journaling/Further Reflection

Ask the Lord to show you how he sees you and journal what he puts on your heart.

Scriptures for Meditation

Psalm 51:3

Proverbs 20:5

Jeremiah 14:20

Luke 15:17

Psalm 51:3

1 Corinthians 13:12

VALUING MYSELF

And should I not be concerned over Nineveh, the great city, in which there are more than a hundred and twenty thousand persons who cannot distinguish their right hand from their left, not to mention the many cattle?

– Jonah 4:11

How common it is for us to find our value in our performance, talents, skills, physical appearance, wealth or status? The scripture at the beginning of this section puts our value in right perspective because it reveals God's perspective. Jonah was sent by God to preach repentance to the Ninevites and, when they did repent and God had mercy, Jonah was angry about it. We take a look at the scripture above and find how God saw them. They were clueless! He said they couldn't tell their left hands from their right hands! That's not a statement of harsh criticism from the Lord, but rather an explanation to Jonah of why he was gentle and didn't smite them like Jonah would have preferred. That clearly reveals the heart of our good shepherd who values his people simply because we are his own.

In Genesis, the serpent tempted Adam and Eve by making them think they weren't good enough and needed to be like gods (Genesis 3:5). Even in our time we hear constant echoes of that moment. Commercials bombard us every day with messages about the myriad ways we are not good enough - how their products can rescue us from teeth that aren't white enough, clothes that aren't bright enough, and vehicles that aren't fast enough, the list goes on. Focusing on the externals to find our value keeps us continually trying to earn what we already have.

Hanging our value on anything other than God's love for us corrupts our vision and becomes how we measure ourselves and the way we believe others see us. When we try to find our worth in people or things other than God's love, we end up hiding and are left thinking if people knew who we really were, they wouldn't accept us. I've known very wealthy people who found their value in their wealth and became paranoid, thinking others only wanted to relate to them for their money. Because their lenses were faulty, it was impossible to convince them otherwise.

Our value is inherent. It can't be earned because we already have it - we are God's children. When we work to prove our value, we're actually placing our worth in something transitory. These can easily become the things we hide behind. Each of us has inherent dignity in the Lord and resting in that fact alleviates so many issues. We no longer have the same self-criticism, arrogance, or condemnation of ourselves or others.

Actually, our confidence becomes unshakeable because it is in God, not in us. This doesn't mean we should stop giving our best effort, but that we should do so from a place of confidence in our okayness, regardless of the outcome. Our performance is no longer an attempt to earn worth, but a gift of gratitude to the Lord for the gifts he's given us. We stop trying to control how things turn out in order to justify our existence. When we have the *being* right, the *doing* flows peacefully and joyfully. The irony is that when we don't spend our valuable time and mental and emotional energy worrying about the outcome, things generally turn out far better. When there is struggle, we are better able to adjust in a healthy way since our focus is on the Lord.

Questions for Reflection and Discussion

1. How do you think not recognizing your inherent value affects your relationships?
2. In what way does not recognizing your inherent value affect how you treat yourself?
3. What are some ways not recognizing your value could affect how you relate to God?
4. How does not recognizing your value affect your spiritual growth?

Prayer

Lord Jesus, we thank you for your cross and Resurrection by which you revealed God's value for each of us. Graciously grant us eyes to see ourselves and each other the way you see us. Let our confidence be in your unshakeable love for each of us. In your holy name we pray. Amen.

Action Step

Think of a person in your life you believe has the highest value. Reflect on the fact that God sees you with far greater worth than this.

Journaling/Further Reflection

Ask the Lord to show you if there are ways you find your value in anything other than him. Ask him what he wants you to know about your value and journal your thoughts.

Scriptures for Meditation

Isaiah 43:1-2

Isaiah 49:16

Jeremiah 31:3

John 3:16

Romans 5:8

1 John 3:1&2

MY BOUNDARIES FOR MYSELF

Talk to yourself like you would to someone you love.

— Brené Brown, Ph.D.

Boundaries are protective limits to ensure safety, health, and right order. They aren't just a right, but a responsibility, because they are an essential component of being good stewards of ourselves. We put gates up in homes with babies and toddlers to protect them from dangerous situations. They also protect caregivers from having to fear for a child's every move. I have a fence up around my yard, which protects my dog from getting lost, stolen, or hit by a car. It also protects me from worrying about her, having to go look for her were she to run off, other people from getting bitten or chased, and drivers from accidentally hitting her. Moreover, it allows her the freedom to go outside without a leash so she can explore and relax in the beautiful outdoors. Boundaries establish rules of engagement and facilitate peace for all parties involved.

Maybe we were never taught that we get to have boundaries for ourselves and so experienced them as hostile walls or as rejection from others. Most people I've talked to didn't have healthy boundaries modeled or set and were never taught how to set them. The reality is that boundaries are essential for healthy relationships. Remember, boundaries will look different for different people, because each of us has unique needs. Boundaries are important in protecting us. They aren't just a right, but a responsibility.

Since we are body, mind, and spirit, we have a need for boundaries in all three of these areas. Are R-rated movies really good for us just because we are older? Just because we can do something doesn't necessarily mean it's conducive to our growth in wholeness and holiness. When we set limits for ourselves, we are keeping the bad out and the good in. Doing so keeps the living waters Jesus wells up within us from being wasted or polluted.

We spend exponentially more time talking to ourselves than we talk to others. That is not to say that we are constantly talking out loud, but our inner voice, thoughts, or expressions can be almost constant. What do we say to ourselves? What does our running commentary sound like? When thoughts that aren't good for us come into our minds about ourselves, others, or situations, what do we do with them? Do we entertain them or do we "take every thought captive in obedience to Christ"? (2 Corinthians 10:5) This is a simple example of setting a healthy boundary in how we relate to ourselves. It is rooted in the boundaries God sets for us in scripture and overflows in our relationship to others.

Considering that God sees us as beloved and precious and values us beyond measure sets a firm foundation for healthy boundaries, which determine the way in which we think about ourselves. Many years ago, I had a job that required an enormous amount of travel. Being on the road so much, I often ate at restaurants. One day I realized when the hostesses would ask me how many were in my party, I regularly answered, "Just one." This may sound like a little thing, but even though I was the one saying it, I felt a sting every time. It felt like the message I was unintentionally sending myself was that my existence was less because I was alone. Instead, I chose to say, "One, please," and that's what I say to this day. Each time I feel an honoring of my dignity as a person, rather than the sense of being diminished, as if I need another's presence to give me significance.

I noticed something similar several years later. Pulling out of the driveway on my way to work, I realized that I had neglected to grab my computer bag or lunch. I caught myself saying out loud and with irritation at myself, "Ugh! I forgot that!" It made me feel frustrated and discouraged. I examined the situation and considered that actually, I had remembered the item before I drove away from the house. Good thing! I changed my message to myself to one of gratitude that I recalled the needed item before I left. This simple change in attitude helped me avoid so much useless frustration at myself. I felt joyful and energized rather than demoralized. Words are powerful. The ones we speak to ourselves regularly shape how we see ourselves, and if we aren't consciously monitoring, our self-talk can often fly in the face of how God sees us. Aligning and realigning our self-concept with the Lord's concept of us is crucial for operating in reality and peace.

Questions for Reflection and Discussion

1. Have you ever thought about the concept of boundaries from yourself that are for yourself?
2. Are there ways you find yourself crossing healthy boundaries in your relation to yourself?

3. What are some ways you relate to yourself that are respectful of healthy boundaries for you?
4. Have you ever noticed how self-talk can affect you?

Prayer

Lord Jesus, we thank you for the immensity of your love. We ask you to give us a healthy understanding of boundaries with ourselves. Please help us to experience them as our cooperation with your loving protection and provision. In your holy name we pray. Amen.

Action Step

What is one thing you say to yourself that you would not say to someone you love? Reflect on that, and practice replacing it with a loving truth.

Journaling/Further Reflection

Spend some time prayerfully considering if you relate to yourself with healthy boundaries. Ask the Lord what he would want you to know about this and journal what he puts on your heart.

Scriptures for Meditation

Psalm 19:14

1 Corinthians 3:16

1 Corinthians 6:19-20

1 Corinthians 10:31

1 Peter 5:7-9

OPENNESS WITH MYSELF

Do not conform yourself to this age but be transformed by the renewal of your mind, that you may discern what is the will of God, what is good and pleasing and perfect.

– Romans 12:2

Like any relationship, your relationship to yourself is a process. When you look at a baby or small child, do you think they have a grasp on the fullness of who they are as an individual? No! Rather, it is through the process of being loved by their parents, discovering their strengths and weaknesses, growing in compassion for others, and beginning to understand who they are to their parents and to God that they begin to know and value themselves, see themselves as gift and learn to return that gift to the Lord. As this happens, their dawning awareness allows them to more consciously participate in God's loving plan and to embrace their baptismal commission as priest, prophet, and king. We don't hit a certain age and suddenly arrive at human, spiritual, or relational maturity. Scripture tells us we are to grow up into the fullness of Christ (Ephesians 4:13). That is a lot of growing to do and it is a long process.

In his book, *Addiction and Grace*[1], psychiatrist and theologian Gerald May says that we all suffer from repression and addiction, which prevent us from responding fully to grace. So, our need to be honest with ourselves is important as we look to move more deeply in connection to God, ourselves, and others. Openness, honesty, and authenticity with ourselves are essential to greater openness to God's mercy, healing, and grace. Realizing how vulnerable that requires us to be also gives us a gentler eye toward our neighbor striving or struggling to do the same.

Since this connection to ourselves is a process, there is no need for discouragement, particularly when we stay rooted in the foundation of connection to God. We're not to grow in self-actualization for the sake of becoming more of ourselves for ourselves alone. Rather, the spiritual journey is about aspiring to drink more deeply of the Living Water of the love of Christ so as to be more transformed into and more intimately united to him. Taking on his mind and his regard of us is part of union with and imitation of him.

Remember, openness with ourselves, like openness with God and others, is a byproduct of the factors of connection. We naturally open up in our relationships when we experience being truly known, valued, and safe. Therefore, if we find honesty with ourselves challenging, we can consider in which of these areas we may be able to relate to ourselves with greater grace so we have the courage needed for greater truth. As a friend of mine often says that any problem is fundamentally a problem between the person and God. Conversely, any healthy formation fundamentally comes from growth in relationship with him. Authenticity doesn't come from being perfect, but in knowing that while imperfect we are perfectly loved.

Questions for Reflection and Discussion

1. Think of someone you've known who seems like they are very comfortable with who they are. Why do you think they are that way? How does it make you feel to be around them?
2. What is the most difficult part of being honest with yourself?

3. Think of a time you were able to be truly open with yourself. How did it turn out? Was there fruit from the experience? If so, what was it?
4. When you struggle with being honest with yourself, what about how God sees you have you usually forgotten or overlooked?

Prayer

Father of light, we ask you to illumine the darkness preventing us from seeing you clearly and ourselves the way you see us. Let your light, Jesus, whom you sent as light of the world, be ever present to us so we may be drawn more closely to you and transformed more perfectly into your image as your children. In Jesus' name we pray. Amen.

Action Step

Ask the Lord to show you an area where he wants to bring you greater truth and grace.

Journaling/Further Reflection

When you think about being open with yourself, authenticity and personal human formation, what stirs within you? Ask the Lord what he wants you to know and note what comes to your mind.

Scriptures for Meditation

Proverbs 11:3

John 8:32

John 16:13

John 17:17

Romans 12:9

2 Corinthians 1:12

BODY, MIND, SPIRIT

May the God of peace himself make you perfectly holy and may you entirely, spirit, soul and body, be preserved blameless for the coming of our Lord Jesus Christ.

– 1 Thessalonians 5:23

God created man. He didn't create spirit, soul, and body separately and then somehow weave them together. In the scripture quote above, St. Paul refers to all three of these aspects as what makes us an entire person. Because of the great expanse of knowledge regarding the different facets of the person, they have become artificially divvied up into distinct areas of study. The truth, however, is there is a continual interplay between them. Maximizing our pursuit of holiness also requires seeking wholeness, and vice versa. We are body, mind, and spirit. We can't opt out of that fact. Spiritual balance and personal wellness require that we tend to all three of these aspects of our person.

The four main hormones that cause us to feel good are dopamine, oxytocin, serotonin, and endorphins. Dopamine is primarily associated with learning new information and accomplishing goals; oxytocin is associated with love, trust, and friendship; serotonin has to do with a sense of respect and importance; and endorphins are released when we push past our physical limits, as in a runner's high – oh, and eating chocolate! Each of these speaks to God's design – in his wisdom, he literally created us for cooperation, collaboration, and connection.

Cortisol is a stress hormone. It is released in times of fear and perceived threat. The release of this hormone shuts down the production of oxytocin, which we said above is necessary to foster trust, friendship, and love. Personal and interpersonal disconnection causes us to exude cortisol. That's a fact of how we are made. This is all the more reason to respect boundaries and relate with compassion. Otherwise, we'll likely fuel stress in ourselves and those around us which will undermine our peace and relationships. Respect and compassion are crucial and perpetuate the cycle of connection from God, through self to others. This is critically important in every cell of our body and is an ongoing factor in every one of our relationships.

We are not at the mercy of our body's use of hormones to keep us on guard. The practice of contemplative prayer has been shown to decrease cortisol. With less cortisol in our bodies, we are more inclined to calmness, compassion, and collaboration, because oxytocin is not reduced. Through such peaceful and loving interaction, mutual respect fosters serotonin because it offers us a sense of importance. We are able to accomplish more, since we are all different members of the body of Christ with varying gifts and skills working together to build the kingdom of God. Thus, the release of dopamine is bolstered. We may even push past our normal physical limits since our interactions are fueling our positive mood and so we receive an endorphin rush. God's design is beautiful. It starts with plugging in through receiving his love in prayer.

There are many facets to wellness for our body, mind, and spirit, and needs vary from person to person, yet some things are consistent. Physically we need good nutrition, hydration, exercise, and sleep. To have a healthy mind, we need to take on the mind of the Lord in all things. To be healthy and grow spiritually we need to be rooted in God's love and truth. We do well to consider in what areas the Lord is calling us to greater health and discipline in each one of these areas; that way we are moving towards ever-greater holiness and wholeness. This is a much more peaceful and effective way to live rather than only seeking solutions when problems arise.

Questions for Reflection/Discussion

1. Have you ever considered that a healthy relationship with God, yourself, and others is a prescription for feeling good? Why do you think that is?
2. Are there areas where you feel the Lord may be nudging you toward greater health in body, mind or spirit?
3. Have there been times when your relationship to you has brought you stress? How so?
4. Have there been times that you've had to consciously choose to have a compassionate response to yourself or another and it's made a difference in a situation? How so?

Prayer

Good and gracious God, thank you for the wisdom with which you made all of creation and particularly for the beauty with which you made our inmost being. You have made us for union with yourself and in that union is our fulfillment, peace, and joy. Please grant us the grace to live in gratitude for your love and to be filled with you, to make you present to all those we meet. We ask this in your holy name. Amen.

Action Step

Spend 10 minutes in prayer with no goal or intention other than focusing on God's infinite and personal love for you.

Journaling/Further Reflection

Reflect on how God has created us to live in wholeness and holiness. If there is anything about that idea you struggle with, ask the Lord what he wants you to know about that.

Scriptures for Meditation

Psalm 139:14

Isaiah 40:28-31

1 Thessalonians 5:23

CONNECTION TO OTHERS

I give you a new commandment: love one another.
As I have loved you, so you also should love one another.

– John 13:34

There can be an imbalance in parenting when a child is taught he's very special, but isn't taught everyone else is, too. This quickly plays itself out in behavioral issues and entitlement. There is a danger in connection to ourselves and the Lord without this third leg of connection to others to balance the tripod. Being called to love and lay down our lives for each other draws us out of the self-centeredness of how special we are and into the trenches of sandpaper ministry, where we are all refined and our rough edges are smoothed. In relationships with others, our weaknesses and woundedness are revealed. It cannot be all giving and no taking, and vice versa. The nature of relationships is reciprocity and we soon find in giving we do receive and sometimes even more than what we are able to contribute. Loving others gives us the experience of being a gift. For such a blessing there is no substitute.

We are created for connection and actually tend toward addictive behavior when we do not have healthy connection with others. British journalist Johann Hari who researched drug addiction, is famously noted as saying, "The opposite of addiction isn't sobriety. The opposite of addiction is connection."[1] This isn't only true in terms of drug and alcohol addiction, but also food, sex, work, and the other many ways we may try to self-medicate. Because God made us to be one in him, lacking community can leave us lacking an experience of unity, and this can leave us feeling unfulfilled.

As we've considered many times so far, the foundation for all relating – relating to ourselves in addition to everyone else – must be a healthy relationship with the Lord. He is the only one who will ever know, value, and be able to protect us perfectly, in this life and in eternity. With this basis in place, we are able to minister and receive his love to each other without anxiety, even in the face of rejection or abandonment. These feelings are very real and human, yet they begin to diminish as we become more rooted in God's constant and unconditional love.

The same pattern that has been revealed in our relationship to God and to ourselves is manifest in our relationships with each other, being known and valued, and the need for boundaries and openness. In the following sections, we'll take a look at those aspects in terms of the give and take in relationship to peers.

Questions for Reflection and Discussion

1. When is a time you felt most connected to another person in a healthy way?
2. How did the factors of being known and valued and having boundaries come into play?
3. Was there give and take in the relationship?
4. Describe how it feels to have connection compared to feeling disconnected.

Prayer

Lord, make me an instrument of your peace.

Where there is hatred, let me sow love.

Where there is injury, pardon.

Where there is doubt, faith.

Where there is despair, hope.

Where there is darkness, light.

Where there is sadness, joy.

O Divine Master,

grant that I may not so much seek to be consoled,

as to console;

to be understood, as to understand;

to be loved, as to love.

For it is in giving that we receive.

It is in pardoning that we are pardoned,

and it is in dying that we are born to eternal life.

Amen.[2]

– St. Francis of Assisi

Action Step

Reflect on friends and peers who have been instruments of grace and peace to you. Think about how they related to you. If possible, reach out to them and thank them for being a gift in your life.

Journaling/Further Reflection

Consider the connection you have to others in your life and ask the Lord to reveal what is healthy, as well as areas for healing and growth. Journal what he lets you know.

Scriptures for Meditation

John 17:21

2 Corinthians 13:11

Galatians 3:28

Ephesians 4:3

Philippians 2:2

1 Peter 3:8

BOUNDARIES FOR OTHERS

Good fences make good neighbors.

– Robert Frost

As a therapist, I've noticed that not many people, at least not many who come to therapy, have been taught good things about boundaries. In fact, some people have been directly or indirectly sent very negative messages about them. Many have been given the idea boundaries are a sign of entitlement, artificial walls, or unhealthy distance. Others have set boundaries only to have them continually criticized and have been shamed for them. Still others have never been taught there is such a thing as setting physical, emotional, and spiritual limits, much less that doing so is a gift for themselves and others. Boundaries play a huge role in healthy communication and relationships.

When discussing or setting boundaries with others, it is best to do so in a time of calm rather than conflict. This makes it easiest for peaceful communication and minimizes the need for defensiveness. People learn to relate to us the way they do based on what boundaries we do or don't establish. When we realize we need to change or establish boundaries with someone, it can be a humbling experience. Being clear is essential, so the other person knows what we are comfortable with and what we aren't. All the while, clarity must be achieved without neglecting charity. That might sound like, "I'm uncomfortable when you say or do (x)." The other person may readily accept your boundary and apologize and then the air is clear. Others may insist on their way and further discussion is needed. Fundamentally, we have a responsibility to communicate how we are okay with being treated and how we aren't. Otherwise, we're relying on others to guess what we're thinking, which is a setup for disaster and is not fair to either party. Most often, people have good intentions and simply aren't aware of our needs. We are all so different.

There may be times when someone may try our boundaries. It may be intentional or unintentional; regardless, we don't have to be upset by such interactions once we are aware of our responsibility to have healthy boundaries. It is natural for people to forget that the boundaries have changed and behave the way they are used to. They may simply need a reminder. The more you see boundaries as a gift for the other person, the more setting and maintaining them becomes easier.

Setting boundaries used to be difficult for me, but over the years it has become much easier. A number of years ago I went to a dentist who tried to pressure me into having elective work done which I didn't want. During a dental appointment, I stated my desire and my rationale. When he pushed the issue at the same visit, I reiterated my wishes. He proceeded to tell his assistant to do a panoramic x-ray of my mouth to see if I was a candidate for the work he was trying to pressure me to have. She put the lead apron over me and was moving the x-ray machine into place. My immediate thought was, "He is older, and a doctor, and so maybe I should do what he's suggesting." Thankfully, that thought only lasted a couple of seconds. The next moment, it came to me that since I am an adult and it is my mouth, I have a right to have my wishes respected. Even if I was wrong, I had the right to be wrong. I respectfully removed the x-ray apron and handed it back to the assistant and very calmly told the doctor it wasn't going to work for me to treat with him. I calmly got up from the chair and left without any drama. That experience was a personal victory and stands out as a positive memory. I learned my safety and peace aren't contingent on the respect others have for my boundaries. The process of deepening connection to God and myself brought me to the point of being able to respond in such a way.

Questions for Reflection and Discussion

1. What messages about boundaries were you sent growing up?
2. How do you feel about setting them?
3. Is it difficult for you to recognize you have a right and a responsibility to set boundaries?
4. Is it difficult for you to set them? Why or why not?

Prayer

Heavenly Father, thank you for calling us your children, and for your faithful, unfailing love. Help us all to know that you desire that we live together in love and peace, and that you give us the grace to bring your kingdom to the world in who we are and what we do each day. We ask this through Christ our Lord. Amen.

Action Step

Oftentimes, anger is a sign that our boundaries, or those of someone we love, have been crossed. If there is an area in your life for which you carry anger, ask the Lord to show you if there is a boundary you need to set or discuss with someone.

Journaling/Further Reflection

For those who have never learned or were sent negative messages about boundaries, setting them and maintaining them can be difficult. Ask the Lord if setting boundaries is an area in which he wants to give you more freedom and grace. Note what comes to mind.

Scriptures for Meditation

Psalm 16:1-11

Proverbs 27:5

Matthew 5:37

1 Corinthians 15:33

Galatians 6:5

Titus 3:10

RESPECTING THE BOUNDARIES OF OTHERS

Do to others whatever you would have them do to you.

This is the law and the prophets.

– Matthew 7:12

Everyone is unique and has their own body, mind, and spirit. Each of us has the responsibility for setting our own boundaries in these areas. We all are required to obey the laws set out by rightful authority (not going against our informed consciences). Within those parameters, we are all called to be good stewards. Our first duty of stewardship is to honor the gift of self that God has given to each of us. Each of us has a different personality, temperament, and life experiences that come together to form who we are in the present moment. Since we are endowed with the dignity of being made in God's image and likeness, each one of us is deserving of respect. We must regard others with the honor with which they are divinely endowed.

Boundaries provide us a sense of self and safety. Simply put, there's a place where we stop and another starts. We don't have the right to cross any lines in regard to another person's body, emotions, or spiritual life. Each person has the indwelling presence of the Blessed Trinity and so is sacred. We need to be invited in by the other person. One lesson I've learned as a therapist is that people are not able to hear answers to questions they haven't yet asked. Trying to force them to do so can do personal and relational damage. The same way we would not desecrate the Eucharist, we ought not violate the boundaries of another, since each person is made in God's own image and likeness and is precious to him.

There are two fundamental emotions: love and fear. Scripture tells us that love drives away fear (1 John 4:18). As we respect the boundaries of others, what they need to feel safe, we are behaving toward that person in a loving way. Even with the best of intentions, we can cross another's boundaries. Unfortunately, this can easily happen in the name of religion. It's easy to convince ourselves that our expression of zeal is for the other person's good. We actually work contrary to his grace in another when we try to force, manipulate, coerce, or guilt them into something. Doing so, especially in God's name, can cause another person to shut down, build walls, or make vows against the godly message or even toward God himself.

It actually makes the most sense to be grateful to others when they have clear boundaries. It lets us know what they need in order to feel safe, respected, and loved, and isn't that how we are called to treat them? It can often be humbling to accept another person's boundaries, but it isn't our job to change them. When we do respect the boundaries another person has set, we are truly valuing that person and not making their worth about our desired result. This fosters true connection and allows us to remain an incarnation of God's love for them, and as such, a vehicle of his grace. It can be difficult to grant each other free will, but in his infinite wisdom that is what God has given each of us. And are we not called to imitate the Lord?

Questions for Reflection and Discussion

1. What are your initial reactions to this section?
2. Are there times you have seen people violate the boundaries of others?

3. Are there times it is difficult for you to not cross another's limits?
4. Was there ever a time it was difficult for you to honor the boundaries of another, but you did it anyway? How did it go?

Prayer

Heavenly Father, we are in awe of your gift of free will. Thank you for showing us how dearly you value our freedom to choose you and the life you have for us. Please give us the grace to imitate you by honoring the freedom of others, so we may be a conduit of your mercy, grace, and love to them. In Jesus' name we pray. Amen.

Action Step

If you have any relationships that are less than peaceful, consider if you respect the boundaries of the other person. If you do not, ask the Lord to show you why doing so is difficult for you and what he wants you to know about it.

Journaling/Further Reflection

Note your thoughts from this section's Action Step. Ask the Lord to show you if there is anything in this area he wants to heal in you and jot down what comes to you, then give him permission to do so.

Scriptures for Meditation

Matthew 7:12

Matthew 19:19

Romans 12:10

Philippians 2:3

2 Peter 1:5-7

1 John 4:11

OPENNESS WITH OTHERS

Let your acquaintances be many,

but one in a thousand your confidant.

- Sirach 6:6

Being open with others is something that requires great courage. Hopefully, by this point, we can begin to put the pieces of connection together and see how they interplay. We have looked at how having a foundation of being known deeply and treasured dearly by God gives us the highest authority upon which to base our identity. Also, we have discussed viewing other people as precious to the Lord and not basing our contentment on their thoughts or actions. It is from this vantage point we can engage with others, knowing their response to us does not make or break us, no matter how truly painful it might be. Another's actions toward us do not affect our value in any way, because we have inherent worth as children of God.

Being able to be vulnerable with another is far easier when we have grown, and continue to grow, in connection to God and ourselves. It's also important to remember that trust is a process. The same way we grow in trust with the Lord and with ourselves, we also grow in our ability to navigate a relationship with another person. This is not accomplished at one time, but is a process that takes time. As discussed, we will generally begin a relationship by sharing something good about ourselves. If we are compassionately received, we may venture into sharing one of our less glorious moments. Perhaps we even come to share an area of hurt, struggle, or shame. This is the process of growing in relationship. Interestingly, scripture actually tells us *not* to trust others (Micah 7:5-6). If we are looking for another person not to fail us, we will be disappointed, because every person is as human as we are. Only God will not break our trust. Instead, we should look for noble intentions and efforts at consistent good will from other people, and understand that there may be times when they fail us out of their own human frailty.

What are the signs that another person wills us good? Does the other person truly know us, or make efforts to do so? Do they treat us in a way that shows us they value us for who we are or do we feel used as a means for them to get their desired goal? Do they respect our physical, emotional, and spiritual boundaries or do they send the message we are not allowed to have limits? If we see red flags in any of these outer layers of connection, we may want to tread the waters of vulnerability very carefully and not have high expectations for healthy connection with them at this time. It may be risky to share sensitive information with them in hopes of being known. Remember when others aren't able to be present to truly hear and see us, recognize our value as children of God, or respect the boundaries we have put in place, often it is not personal. Rather, it is a reflection of what they're capable of at the time.

Finally, in all peer relationships, there ought to be reciprocity – give and take. It doesn't mean we keep score, and certainly some days are better than others. Patience and understanding with others is essential. We don't want to engage with others with a constant scrutiny of every interaction, the same way we would fail if we were judged so harshly. Given the ebb and flow of life and circumstances, these factors of connection can be guidelines to help us avoid drama and hurt in relationships. With practice we will grow in greater peace and fulfillment from the Lord's indwelling presence, and that which we receive will flow from us out to others.

Questions for Reflection and Discussion

1. Is it helpful to you to consider the factors of connection in navigating openness with others? In what way?
2. Think of someone who has proven themselves trustworthy to you. Do you see the factors of healthy connection present in your relationship?
3. In what way are the factors of connection (known, valued, boundaries, openness) helpful in assessing a person's trustworthiness?
4. In what way can you see growing in connection to God and self contributes to your ability to be open with others?

Prayer

Lord Jesus, you made yourself completely vulnerable to us in taking on our humanity, suffering and dying for us, and coming to us in the Eucharist. Please give us the grace to find our firm foundation in you. Grace us with the courage and wisdom to grow in holiness and healthy relationships. Thank you for your presence in our lives, drawing us closer to you each day. In your holy name we pray. Amen.

Action Step

Consider a relationship in which you might have difficulty trusting. Think about the factors for healthy connection, what might be lacking? Ask the Lord to show you what he wants you to know about this.

Journaling/Further Reflection

Ask the Lord to show you what he wants you to know about your openness to others and note what comes to you.

Scriptures for Meditation

Ecclesiastes 4

Sirach 6:5-17

OPENNESS FROM OTHERS

> *By having a reverence for life, we enter into a spiritual relation with the world. By practicing reverence for life, we become good, deep, and alive.*
>
> – Albert Schweitzer

A number of years ago, I was supervising a team of therapists and at the end of the workday I received a call from one of them wanting to consult about a teenager she was treating in a weeklong intensive program. The therapist said she didn't think the child was appropriate for the week of treatment and thought she would need more time to build rapport. She told me for their three-hour session that day the girl had insisted she didn't believe in emotions. She said that she thought they were an artificial idea human beings had invented. The teen very much needed intensive trauma work. Sadly, she had been in counseling for over a decade at that point, all with little benefit.

I asked the therapist if she would mind if I attended their session the next day. She readily agreed. When the client came into the room and saw me with her therapist her eyes widened. She thought she was in trouble. I simply said I was her therapist's supervisor, and I had heard they had a difficult session the day before and wanted to see if I could help. I told her I had gone through the same treatment years prior, expecting no relief, and instead was greatly helped. I went on to add that I had looked at her chart and knew she'd been in therapy since she was a toddler, which meant we, as mental health professionals, had failed her or she wouldn't still be struggling so. I added that I couldn't imagine she would want to tell her story to one more person. She sat still and silent. Finally, she asked, "Are you a unicorn?" I had no idea what she meant. She said, "You came skipping in here throwing trauma sprinkles and rainbows and suddenly I want to do this." I realized she was connecting to me and so I knew I needed to spend a few more minutes casually chatting with her and her therapist to get them comfortable with each other before I left the room so they could get to work.

What I learned from that experience is that openness is a byproduct. It can't be a goal. The young therapist was so interested in the client cooperating with treatment that she was, metaphorically, attempting to bash the young lady's door down, forcing her to accept it. She was asking her to be open, but all the while, she was sending the message that she would have value if only she would participate in the therapy. On the other hand, I hadn't used a technique of some sort on her. I was simply relating to her the way I would have wanted to be treated. If I wanted her to be honest, it only made sense that I be honest, too. In expressing to her that I understood her, acknowledged her value regardless of if she chose to participate in the program, and respected her boundaries, she readily opened her heart and ended up doing fantastic work through the rest of the week.

It would be a drastically different story if I had gone into the treatment room and said the same things but with the goal of getting her to cooperate, as opposed to the goal of connecting. She, most likely, would have been able to sense a lack of consistency or sincerity and would have walled off her heart, and all for good reason. I wouldn't have been trustworthy if I had made treatment a goal. She had to be the goal. I had to surrender potential failure in front of one of my team, but it didn't matter. I couldn't matter at that point – not to her. I had to know I mattered to the Lord and to myself. It was my job to communicate that she mattered. I didn't really fully understand how important what I was doing was and didn't know why she so quickly decided to engage in treatment until I prayed about it after the session. Through that meeting, the Lord taught me openness is a byproduct rather than an end in and of itself. That lesson changed how I aspire to relate.

Whether or not others choose to open at a given time or in a particular circumstance, reverencing them is an honor because it is an opportunity to imitate how the Lord relates to us. When others do open up to us, it is profound and humbling and deserves to be met with reverence and respect.

Questions for Reflection and Discussion

1. How do you feel when others aren't open with you?
2. How do you feel when others are open with you?
3. Can you see how openness is a byproduct of the conditions of connection (boundaries, valued and known)? Have you ever had a similar experience?

Prayer

Lord Jesus, we thank you for the opportunity to reverence others the way you do. Please help us to use each opportunity to communicate your love for others by how we treat them. Please help us to show the same patience and understanding to others that you so tenderly show to us. In your holy name we pray. Amen.

Action Step

Take advantage of time in a store, restaurant, or gathering and note what fosters openness among people and what tends to shut people down. See if you notice how boundaries, acceptance (value) and being known come into play.

Journaling/Further Reflection

Ask the Lord to show you what he wants you to know about reverencing others when they are open with you and journal your thoughts.

Scriptures for Meditation

Proverbs 21:21

Proverbs 22:2

Luke 6:30

Romans 12:10

Ephesians 5:21

1 John 4:7-12

VALUING & BEING VALUED

Human dignity is the same for all human beings: when I trample on the dignity of another, I am trampling on my own.

— Pope Francis

To value another the way God values them means seeing them as they truly are, a treasure of immeasurable worth. People are not a means to an end. In other words, whether we agree or disagree with someone has nothing to do with their inherent value. I could disagree with someone's opinions, beliefs, or actions, but it shouldn't change the acceptance I have for them as a human being and the dignity with which I regard them. Remember, our dignity comes from the fact that God is who he is and that he showed his value for us when he purchased us with the price of his own Son.

It's amazing what happens when we begin to see others in this light. It actually begins to change how we view ourselves. Suddenly, we're more capable of realizing our own worth is unwavering. It doesn't matter if we are right or wrong, perfect or imperfect. Reminding ourselves that our neighbor's value doesn't change helps us recognize the same is true of us. We begin to accept that truth at a deeper level. Recognizing this about others affords us greater objectivity and, in the long run, the lesson blesses our view of ourselves, as well. In a very real way, we begin to see the circumstances of the day as scenery on the journey to an ever-deepening reception of God's gift of himself. Less and less is offensive. Less and less disturbs our peace. More and more is recognized as gift until all is seen as a personal, intimate self-gift of God.

There's an ironic consequence of treating people with value regardless of if they agree or cooperate with us. It's that they begin to agree and cooperate a lot more. When we are treated like our value is contingent on someone's approval of us, it can cause us to shut down because that estimation is fundamentally not true and we know it intuitively, even if we don't know it consciously. Remember, openness is a byproduct of having our boundaries respected, being valued, and being seen as good. We cannot make cooperation the goal. To do so sabotages the very point; we all have the same value no matter what.

Regardless of our best efforts, we can't make each other feel valued and accepted. Once I worked with a client who was completely convinced I was judging and rejecting her. It couldn't have been further from the truth. I had actually struggled with some things in very much the same way she did and felt great compassion for her. It pained me not to be able to alleviate her pain caused by her belief that I saw her with condemnation, but it was not within my ability to do so. The issue was the lenses through which she viewed herself. I had to stay in the place of being accepting and fight the temptation to try to control her. To force my acceptance on her would have violated her boundaries and would have been fighting a losing battle. It was helpful to remind myself that she could only connect with me to the extent she was connected to herself. In situations like that, we can trust that the Lord loves the other person way more than we possibly could and his ability to heal is infinitely greater.

Questions for Reflection and Discussion

1. What are some ways we can communicate to another person recognition of their value?
2. What's a time or circumstance in which you've struggled to see someone's unchanging value?
3. Is there a time you treated someone with value when it was difficult to do so? What was it like?
4. What best communicates to you that another recognizes your unchanging worth?

Prayer

Dear Lord, we thank you for your death and resurrection, by which you showed us your value for us. Please give us your heart to see how precious every person is in your sight and the grace to treat them accordingly, regardless of the cost. In your holy name we pray. Amen.

Action Step

Consider a person with whom you currently struggle or have struggled in the past. Ask the Lord to show you if it is because you are placing their value on a particular response from them.

Journaling/Further Reflection

Ask the Lord to show you if there is anything blocking you from valuing others as he does and why that is. Journal what he reveals to you.

Scriptures for Meditation

We draw first on the Lord's knowledge and value of us and seek to imitate him in relating to others. Notice the scriptures for meditation are the same ones from the section regarding God's value of us.

Isaiah 43:4

Matthew 6:25-34

Luke 12:6-7

John 3:16

Romans 8:28

Titus 3:4-7

KNOWING & BEING KNOWN

People don't care how much you know

until they know how much you care.

– Theodore Roosevelt

In choosing how we relate to others, we start at the heart, that is, we start with believing the other to be very good and made in God's image and likeness. This is a central tenet of our faith as Catholics and is the heart of our respect for human life. As human beings, we are all works in progress. Since this is the truth of the Lord's relationship to us, why would it be any less true for someone else? If we stop at the fact that he sees us this way and don't extend the same to others, we risk being egocentric and arrogant. We also call into question how much we believe in God's unchanging love for us. Very quickly, we can become either an idol or insecure in the Lord's love. Looking at others with God's view creates in us a capacity for empathy, reverence, and respect of the other that we cannot attain any other way. This is a part of taking on God's mind for creation.

The quote from Scottish author and theologian Ian Maclaren, "Be pitiful, for every man is fighting a hard battle,"[1] encourages us to imitate how the Lord relates to each of us. Unfortunately, it's too easy to assume we know what is going on with a person based on what we perceive on the outside. If we are going to look for a fundamental truth to guide our interactions with others, this is the safest one; we cannot possibly know what is going on inside a person based on their exterior. Many times we are not even fully aware of what is operating within us on the deepest level.

We relate to the people in our lives with differing degrees of intimacy and yet we can communicate the concept of knowing others as very good in simple yet powerful ways. If you don't already do this, the next time you go to a store or a restaurant, look the person who is assisting you in the eye with the mindset that they are a person *performing* a service, not the service itself. They are not a means to an end. Smile. Ask them how they're doing and truly listen to their response. It's amazing how much a person is touched by being seen and heard as an individual.

We all need to be known and as we've discussed, healthy boundaries help us to safely navigate this. Remember our focus should be on *being* rather than *doing*. The same way the Lord called the apostles to be fishers of men, rather than to do the catching, it is our responsibility to see and hear others. We can't necessarily make someone feel seen and heard or known to be very good. How another will respond to us is a matter of their view of themselves. What we can do is that which God has called us to, to reverence them and see them for the valued creation they are. This fosters connection, but we can only do our part.

Questions for Reflection and Discussion

1. What strikes you most from this section?
2. Is it difficult or easy for you to see others with empathy?
3. Have you ever related to clerks or wait staff as individual and treasured, and not a means to an end? How did that go?
4. What changes in you when you see, realize, or recognize that others are fighting a great battle in their lives? Especially if that battle isn't visible from the outside?

Prayer

Heavenly Father, you who created us all in your image and likeness, please grant us your eyes through which to see our neighbor. May your love flow to them through your loving gaze. In Jesus' name we pray. Amen.

Action Step

Take an extra moment in a transaction or interaction this week to truly see and hear the person assisting you as a person rather than a function or service.

Journaling/Further Reflection

Ask the Lord to show you times it's more difficult to see others with empathy and then ask him what he wants you to know about that. Note what comes to you.

Scriptures for Meditation

We draw first on the Lord's knowledge and value of us and seek to imitate him in relating to others. Notice the scriptures from this section regarding God's knowledge of us are also used for meditation.

Jeremiah 1:5

Nahum 1:7

Psalm 139

John 10:14

John 10:27

HEALTHY COMMUNICATION

The fool takes no delight in understanding,

but rather in displaying what he thinks.

– Proverbs 18:2

First, let's sum up what we've learned about connection so far. We all need an authentic sense of safety, respect, and being known as good in order to facilitate openness. Putting this information to use, we have a solid foundation for communication. Regardless of the subject matter for verbal dialogue, these are ever present needs in people. Because they are invisible and because we have the same needs, we tend to ignore them and press ahead into talking, all the while neglecting the conversation running in the background.

Am I safe? Am I accepted as I am? Am I seen and heard as an individual who is good? These questions are the litmus test we generally use to assess how safe it is for us to open up, become vulnerable, and share our inmost selves. We need to start by plugging into God for the affirmation of who we are in him and strive to accept this truth more deeply. This is our mode from which we will receive what others present to us. When we begin a conversation with another after having first adjusted our vision of the Lord and ourselves in him, we are better able to approach the other calmly and with compassion.

Of course, we cannot control if others are doing the same, but we can do our part to ease the communication process by keeping in mind that others have the same needs for safety, respect and acceptance. So, it is important to communicate these and to be present to truly see and hear them, not just their words. Here are the things we can do:

- Safety and Respect – shown by awareness of and honoring a person's boundaries. Being gentle with our words, tone, and body language are all important since we communicate in all three of these ways.
- Valuing and Accepting – don't make the other person's worth, even in your mind and heart, about the outcome of the conversation. When our peace seems contingent on the response from the other person, we need to focus more on the

Lord before engaging. He is our prince of peace. Nothing anyone else says or doesn't say can make or break us.

- <u>Validate</u> – acknowledge the other person's view and/or difficulty. This doesn't mean we have to agree with them, but we can agree and recognize their struggle.
- <u>Be gentle; Smile</u> (if appropriate) – this may sound remedial, but it's a way to remind them, and us, that they are of unfathomable worth.
- <u>Make eye contact</u> – this helps to communicate that we are paying attention.
- <u>Don't multitask</u> – not being distracted by phone or activities sends the message that we value the other.

Remember to practice these activities and thoughts in your own life, and begin to see how your relationships flourish because of them. Furthermore, healthy communication is greatly facilitated when we have a common language and framework from which to approach it. Consider sharing this book with your family, friends, groups, teams, or community so that you can begin to bring some equilibrium and common understanding to the way in which the relationships in your life develop and grow.

Questions for Reflection and Discussion

1. What unspoken concern do you notice the most within yourself prior to a challenging conversation?
2. Which, if any, of the positive tips above do you naturally find to be a part of how you relate to others?
3. Which, if any, of the positive tips do you find most helpful to consider when others relate to you?
4. In what ways do you believe a common understanding of connection would make for more peaceful relating with friends? In families? In communities?

Prayer

Lord Jesus, you prayed we would all be one in you. Please grant us the grace to experience your mercy and love toward us and to be instruments of that same mercy and love to others. In your holy name we pray. Amen.

Action Step

Practice implementing the tips above in your daily conversations with others.

Journaling/Further Reflection

Ask the Lord to show you what is most difficult for you in relating to others and what he wants you to know. Note what he puts on your heart.

Scriptures for Meditation

Proverbs 18:2

Proverbs 18:13

Matthew 18:15

Ephesians 4:15

Ephesians 4:29

James 1:19

NAVIGATING RELATIONAL STRUGGLES

For where two or three are gathered together

in my name, there am I in the midst of them.

– Matthew 18:20

As surely as we have the indwelling presence of the Holy Trinity through baptism, we are meant to be occasions of grace for each other. Since it is our call to be incarnations of God, his hands and feet in the world at this time, even our simple interactions can minister his love, mercy, and healing. Yet, life can be complex and, of course, we all come with different temperaments, personalities, histories, and preferences. There are a great many moving parts that make up who we are.

Because of this, two or more people gathering often present challenges. But notice that, in the scripture above, they have drawn together in Jesus' name, to enter into his presence. Considering what characterizes how the Lord relates to us, we know he engages with us through seeing and hearing us as uniquely good and that he cherishes us and respects the free will he's given us. In short, he longs and seeks to relate to us with the deepest connection. Actually, we are made not just for communion, but for *union* with him. We gather in his name when we imitate his example. When we hit speed bumps and rough patches in relating, it is helpful to go back to these basics. In openly seeking to see and hear each other as uniquely good and cherished, we are able to not just *go* through tough times, but to *grow* through them as individuals and in communion with each other.

Years ago I taught these connection principles to a 16-year-old boy and his mother. They're so simple, he was quickly able to grasp them. We used them each week to gain insight into his relational struggles with his parents and peers. After only a couple of weeks, he could explain how he was using these concepts to assess interactions in his relationships, and when something felt off he was able to get right back on course. He and his mother began to work together to calmly examine difficulties they were experiencing and peacefully arrive at understandings. Their relationship began to flourish. Beginning with a mutual understanding that they were both seeking connection made a world of difference. Suddenly, defenses were dropped and they were able to examine circumstances together. They had attitudes of collaboration because they understood they had a common goal, common needs, and rules of engagement.

Questions for Reflection and Discussion

1. In reflecting on a time you've experienced difficulty in a relationship, which connection principle(s) was/were lacking?
2. When you've had peaceful relationships, can you see that the connection principles were present?
3. What are your thoughts about having the connection principles as a shared approach with family, friends, or coworkers? What difficulties or benefits do you foresee?

Prayer

Good and gracious God, you endow us with the great gift of ministering your life and love to each other. Please grant us the grace to receive this grace humbly and to live it faithfully. We ask this in the name of our Lord Jesus Christ. Amen.

Action Step

If you haven't already, share this understanding of connection with someone.

Journaling/Further Reflection

Ask the Lord to show you which of the factors for connection most often negatively affects your relationships and is most in need of his healing. Ask him what he wants you to know and invite him into that area. Record what he lets you know.

Scriptures for Meditation

1 Corinthians 13:4-5

Ephesians 4:2

Colossians 3:13-14

1 Peter 4:8

1 John 3:18

1 John 4:18

PSEUDO-CONNECTION

Do you not know that you are the temple of God, and that the Spirit of God dwells in you? If anyone destroys God's temple, God will destroy that person; for the temple of God, which you are, is holy.

— 1 Corinthians 3:16-17

Since reciprocity between people in the areas of connection (boundaries, valued, known and openness) is essential for healthy and holy relationships, it stands to reason a lack of give and take in these areas leads to unhealthy and even abusive relationships. For example, in any type of abuse, there are boundary violations of a physical, emotional, and/or spiritual nature. In pornography, for example, there is no reciprocity; instead God's boundaries for another are exploited, while their value is reduced to use, and their personhood is disregarded. Also, the one viewing pornography violates their own dignity and God's protective limits for themselves.

There are a wide variety of ways we can attempt to satisfy our desire for connection with God, ourselves, and others in life-giving and life-affirming ways. Food, shopping, drugs, alcohol, sex, excessive work, are just some examples. For a brief moment they may distract from our hunger for authentic connection, but in the long run they fail to satisfy and their fruits are internal and external discord rather than peace and love. I attended a talk a number of years ago by Vincent Felitti, M.D., about the effects of adverse childhood experiences. In discussing the attempt to drown out the residual internal pain from early traumas with substances he said, "You can never get enough of what almost works." The same is true of attempts to use a substitute for the innate need to connect. We would never be able to get enough of what might *almost* work. We would end up chasing faulty remedies and create cycles of frustration and internal and/or relational conflict.

Often, there is much talk about chastity among teens in religious circles. While this is an important value, it's also important to teach young people how to connect in a healthy way. Sexually immoral behavior is, oftentimes, a desire to connect acted out in uneducated, immature, or wounded ways. Given that we are made for connection, we need to learn, practice and teach healthy connection so relationships are truly fulfilling, leading to the wholeness and holiness the Lord wants for us all.

The more we grow in healthy connection, the more we are set free from bondage and decay, and grow in the freedom God intends for us as his children. We can begin to recognize the factors of connection in peace and their absence in conflict and so learn to calibrate our internal meter during times of struggle. It is difficult, if not impossible, to think of a human suffering that can't be traced back to a breakdown in connection. Once we identify the relationship where the gap is, we are well on our way to knowing how to direct our efforts towards peace.

Questions for Reflection and Discussion

1. What examples of pseudo-connection come to mind or have you experienced?
2. In your answer from above, which connection factors are missing or violated?

3. Are there ways that recognizing the factors of connection have benefited you already? If yes, how so?

Prayer

Heavenly Father, we thank you for the beauty with which you have endowed every human soul. Please grace us with your eyes to always see you in everyone. In Jesus' name we pray. Amen.

Action Step

If there are areas of struggle in your life, spend some time considering if the root is in lack of connection to yourself, the Lord, or others, and what factor(s) of connection might be missing.

Journaling/Further Reflection

Ask the Lord what he wants you to know about your answer from the action step above and note what he puts on your heart.

Scriptures for Meditation

Matthew 18:5&6

1 Corinthians 6:19-20

Galatians 5:19-21

Hebrews 13:3

James 4:1-17

CONCLUSION

Establishing a foundation of peace and fulfillment in life, physically, emotionally, and spiritually, is a matter of delving more deeply into the reality of God's connection to us. Fully receiving and being transformed by the indwelling presence of the Blessed Trinity is an ongoing process. Faith in God's love for us becomes more surely our source of confidence and self-worth, hope in him becomes our foundation of joy no matter what may come our way, and his love is our unfathomable fulfillment "packed together, shaken down, and overflowing" (Luke 6:38) that overflows into the lives of others. The more we grow in wholeness, the more we pursue holiness unencumbered. As we grow in holiness, our personal integration and interpersonal relationships become more peaceful. It all starts with receiving from the Lord, as he has first loved us (1 John 4:10). However, recall that our relationship to ourselves is our mode, the lens that influences our ability to perceive him clearly.

Seeking health in our physical, emotional, and spiritual lives is interwoven, since those aspects of our person are interwoven. This quest is a beautiful collaboration with God's perfect plan and redeeming grace as we endeavor, in as much as is our part, to prepare a greater dwelling place for him in our hearts. As our capacity for him increases, his presence progressively fills and permeates us, setting into motion a metamorphosis that transforms all we do. This is what will heal each wounded heart, convert each wayward desire, and unite families, peoples, and nations as the bride of Christ.

SPECIAL NOTE

The dynamics of connection discussed in this book treat relationships between peers and colleagues. It works a bit differently when the relationship is between parents and children, or people in authority and those they are to serve, or to whom they are called to minister, because reciprocity is not the same.

APPENDIX

This video gives a great explanation of the biology behind how God created us for connection. The social brain and its superpowers: Matthew Lieberman, Ph.D. at TEDxStLouis.
https://www.youtube.com/watch?v=NNhk3owF7RQ.

In this short clip, Brené Brown, Ph.D. provides a simple explanation of the power of empathy in communication.
https://www.youtube.com/watch?v=1Evwgu369Jw.

Follow the link below to learn more about the importance of boundaries in interpersonal dynamics. Boundaries with Brené Brown, Ph.D. https://www.youtube.com/watch?v=5U3VcgUzqiI.

This homily by Fr. Dave Pivonka, TOR is an inspiring look into the healing and transforming power of being known by the Lord. Fr. Dave Pivonka, TOR - Sunday Homily: 2016 Steubenville Power and Purpose Conference
https://www.youtube.com/watch?v=c5_AdFmck-w.

A modern adaptation of the renowned poem "The Hound of Heaven," by Francis Thompson, is a moving description of opening our hearts to God and embracing his boundaries for our lives.
The Hound of Heaven A Modern Adaptation
https://www.youtube.com/watch?v=RXlgz4aBKt8

The Key to an Abundant Life

by Margaret Mary Vasquez, LPCC-S

Jesus came so that we might have abundant life (John 10:10) and yet that type of life seems quite elusive to many of us, whether often or from time to time. Sometimes even the desire for life itself is lost. Why is that? Was there a lack in his provision or in our ability to receive the abundance he has to offer? Have other people or circumstances stolen it? Is that possible? Where is it and how do we get it? In answering these questions, we can restore your birthright of life in abundance.

Let's go back to the start of things. In the beginning God created. Why? It couldn't be because he was bored, needed to be loved, worshipped, or served. He doesn't need. He is the essence of fullness, wholeness, and completeness. He created because he is love and love flows outward. In the creation accounts we get to hear God's conversation with himself, the Trinity. Let's listen to what he says. As we eavesdrop, we hear him say, "Let us make man in our image, after our likeness" (Genesis 1:26). The giving that occurs in the love of the Trinity is superabundant and overflows into creation.

It is manifest in the vastness, vividness, and wildness of the animals, ocean, sky, and land, but that is not enough. He desires to give away his very self and so created them male and female (Genesis 1:27) to receive different aspects of the Trinity and to reflect those aspects.

The truth is, we are made in and from and for an overflow of the infinite love of the Trinity. We are conceived in that family. No conception is an accident, unintended, or unwanted. His creative love, which is his very self, is purposeful, giving, and profuse. We really could stop there and soak in that reality for all eternity and still only begin to absorb it, since he is infinite and we can never contain him. Colossians 1:17 tells us that he holds us together in himself. If it weren't so, we would be rent asunder. His love, or rather his self, is far too powerful. We have his indwelling presence to receive him, as our capacity is altogether too tiny. How completely intimate, humbling, and mind-blowing it is that we get to stand in front of such a fire hose of Love as his grace and mercy rush into, through us, into him, and back again.

Don't be afraid that you'll grow selfish or self-centered if you take this time to drink him in, because that is not how his love, true love, works. Don't worry if you find vast room for growth in your ability to absorb his love. Establishing a foundation is a process. His love is meant to flow through us, not just into us, but don't rush out your door to help your neighbor the second you begin to understand the love of the Trinity. Love of neighbor will come in due time. You need to be nourished first, at least that's how God sees it, and he is the biggest proponent of charity you could ever imagine. In being called to imitate God, we are not called to *do* charity, but to *be* charitable. Just as Thomas of Celano said, Saint Francis of Assisi didn't so much pray as he became a prayer.[1] Likewise, we are not so much called to *do* loving things, but rather to *be* love.

What does it mean that God is love and pours himself into you? It means that you are loved first. 1 John 4:10 makes this clear: "In this is love: not that we have loved God, but that he loved us and sent his Son as expiation for our sins." He is the Alpha. His love is the starting point, not mine. Our love is not self-generated. He has to be the source, as he is love itself. I cannot be the source of love and if it is of my own love that I am giving, I am empty before I start. You started with being loved, held together by love and with an indwelling of love always, even before you were, even before you ever longed for love. You had the complete and personal attention of the omnipotent, awesome one even before you existed. It is he who brought you into existence. Your creation was his initiative and an overflow of himself. If you want to know who you are, you are a child of God, a child of he who is love. You are a far greater manifestation of him than the mountains, seas, flowers, and sunrise. His passion for you does not change and cannot be lost. You are an outflow of his self, as his child. His love for you, his self for you, is unconditional. He is unchanging and unwaveringly for you. In his infinite power and wisdom, he is loving you in and through every moment and every circumstance. No tear, no pain has gone unseen by his eyes and unfelt by his heart. He will reward all in eternity.

Let's not skip from that love to love of neighbor. If we do, we lose the key. John 13:34 says, "As I have loved you, so you also should love one another" and so tells us the manner in which to love our neighbor. Mark 12:31 gives us the secret of how to let the love of God flow through us: "You shall love your neighbor as yourself." The key is to love ourselves. You are called to love yourself the same way God loves you, unconditionally, compassionately, and mercifully. Then and only then are we in a place of being truly in

God, who is love, and where God, who is love, is able to flow through us. From that place, love naturally flows out from us to others without an angle or ulterior motive.

    You were not made to do good things. You are called to be a manifestation of God's goodness. That is it. Those are the facts, pure and simple. Unfortunately, many of us get a different message from our parents or early caregivers. It's sadly rare to find the person who did not learn some degree of a quid pro quo of acceptance and approval as a child. For many of us, acceptance and approval were not bedrock, but only given as rewards for particular behavior – high grades, exceptional performance in sports or the arts, and the like. How is a child supposed to experience God's love as unconditional when the people meant to image God's provision, protection, tenderness, and nurturance show us something else in the day-to-day? Their own brokenness and experience of conditional love keeps the cycle going and passes it down from generation to generation. We then emerge from childhood with an experience of life that flies in the face of the all-powerful, unconditional, unalterable love of God. We are perfectly poised to enter adulthood from a place of emotional debt, if not bankruptcy, and we take up a side job of doing things to try to earn that absolute, unfailing love that we already have, but do not experience.

If heart knowledge of God's passionate and all consuming eternal romance with you is not the foundation of your self-concept, go back to the beginning. He is outside of time. He is then and he is now all at once, overflowing with such passion at the thought of you that you sprang into being and are sustained in your cherished existence. Know that his passion for you has not changed in the least, the passion is HIM. God IS love. God is FOR you from the beginning, through every moment and forever. Be not afraid.

NOTES

Connection Overview
1. Turton, W.H. "Thou, Who at thy First Eucharist didst Pray", Hymnary.org, 2007. hymnary.org/text/lord_who_at_thy_first_eucharist_didst_pr.

2. John Paul II. "Fides et Ratio." The Holy See, 14 Sept. 1998, w2.vatican.va/content/john-paulii/en/encyclicals/documents/hf_jp_ii_enc_14091998_fides-et-ratio.html.

3. Lieberman, Matthew. *The Social Brain and Its Superpowers.* YouTube. TED video, 2013. https://www.youtube.com/watch?v=NNhk3owF7RQ.

4. Todd, Rev. Wilmer L. "The Disposition of the Receiver Determines the Message Received." The Lafourche Gazette, March 3, 2020. https://www.lafourchegazette.com/columns/what_a_life/the-disposition-of-the-receiver-determines-the-message-received/article_18be4266-60b5-5ede-94b0-b74e4d595f3e.html.

Connection to God
1. Catholic, Church. *Catechism of the Catholic Church: Revised in accordance with the official Latin text promulgated by Pope John Paul II (2nd ed.).* Washington, D.C.: United States Catholic Conference, 1997.

Prayer
1. Cross, John of the. "Ascent of Mt. Carmel." Essay. In The Collected Works of St. John of the Cross, 86–86. Washington, D.C., Washington, D.C.: Institute of Carmelite Studies, 2017.

God Provides Boundaries
1. Cressy, Serenus. *XVI Revelations Of Divine Love, Shewed to a Devout Servant of Our Lord, Called Mother Juliana, An Anchorite of Norwich: Who Lived in the Days of King Edward the Third.* London, England: R.F.S., 1670.

Openness with God
1. ThoughtCo. *Learn the Words to the Catholic Prayer, 'Come, Holy Spirit'.* Learn Religions, Aug. 25, 2020, learnreligions.com/come-holy-spirit-prayer-542615.

Knowing God
1. Asbury, C., Mabury, P., & Ingram, J. Reckless love. Bethel Music, 2017.

Embracing God's Boundaries
1. Ball, S. *Our Lady of Lourdes: A Message For Times Like This.* CALLED TO TRADITION, 2020. https://www.calledtotradition.com/seth/our-lady-of-lourdes-a-message-for-times-like-this.

2. Delio, I. *Crucified love: Bonaventure's mysticism of the crucified Christ.* Franciscan Press, 1998.

3. Wintz, J. *Saint Francis' Prayer before the Crucifix.* Franciscan Media, 2020. https://www.franciscanmedia.org/franciscan-spirit-blog/saint-francis-prayer-before-the-crucifix.

Going Deeper
1. Marie, B. A. *Grace Perfects Nature.* 2008, Catholicism.org. https://catholicism.org/grace-perfects-nature.html.

Connection to Self
1. Todd, Rev. Wilmer L. "The Disposition of the Receiver Determines the Message Received." The Lafourche Gazette, March 3, 2020. https://www.lafourchegazette.com/columns/what_a_life/the-disposition-of-the-receiver-determines-the-message-received/article_18be4266-60b5-5ede-94b0-b74e4d595f3e.html.

Knowing Myself
1. Cressy, Serenus. *XVI Revelations Of Divine Love, Shewed to a Devout Servant of Our Lord, Called Mother Juliana, An Anchorite of Norwich: Who Lived in the Days of King Edward the Third.* London, England: R.F.S., 1670.

2. VonSchlegel, Katharina. "Be Still My Soul". Amazing Hymns, 2021. https://amazinghymns.com/be-still-my-soul.

Openness with Myself
1. May, G. G. *Addiction and Grace: Love and Spirituality in the Healing of Addictions.* HarperSanFrancisco, 2007.

Connection to Others
1. Hari, J. *Everything You Think You Know About Addiction is Wrong.* TED, 2015. https://www.ted.com/talks/johann_hari_everything_you_think_you_know_about_addiction_is_wrong.

. 2. Francis, Giuliano Ferri, and Elio Sala. *The Prayer of St. Francis.* 2013. Print.

Knowing and Being Known
1. MacLaren, Ian. *Afterwards and Other Stories.* N.p.: CreateSpace Independent Publishing Platform, 2017.

Appendix
"The Key to an Abundant Life"
1. Francis, Bergogelio, and Alicia von Stamwitz. *The Spirit of Saint Francis: Inspiring Words from Pope Francis.* Cincinnati, Ohio: Franciscan Media, 2015.

RESOURCES

Alexander, J. F. *I Am Sophia: a Novel*. Eugene, Oregon: Resource Publications, 2021.

Augustine, Saint. *The Confessions of St. Augustine; The Imitation of Christ*. New York, New York: P. F. Collier & son, 1909.

Asbury, C., Mabury, P., & Ingram, J. Reckless love. Bethel Music, 2017.

Ball, S. *Our Lady of Lourdes: A Message For Times Like This*. CALLED TO TRADITION, 2020. https://www.calledtotradition.com/seth/our-lady-of-lourdes-a-message-for-times-like-this.

Boersma, H. *Seeing God: The Beatific Vision in Christian Tradition*. W B EERDMANS PUB CO, 2018.

Bright, Tania. *Don't Beat Yourself up: Learning the Wisdom of Kindsight*. Oxford, England: Monarch Books, 2015.

Catholic, Church. *Catechism of the Catholic Church: Revised in accordance with the official Latin text promulgated by Pope John Paul II (2nd ed.)*. Washington, D.C.: United States Catholic Conference, 1997.

Croiset, John. *The Devotion to the Sacred Heart*. Tan, 1988.

Cross, John of the. "Ascent of Mt. Carmel." Essay. In The Collected Works of St. John of the Cross, 86–86. Washington, D.C., Washington, D.C.: Institute of Carmelite Studies, 2017.

Cressy, Serenus. *XVI Revelations Of Divine Love, Shewed to a Devout Servant of Our Lord, Called Mother Juliana, An Anchorite of Norwich: Who Lived in the Days of King Edward the Third*. London, England: R.F.S., 1670.

Delio, I. *Crucified love: Bonaventure's mysticism of the crucified Christ*. Franciscan Press, 1998.

Edenfield, T. M., & Saeed, S. A. *An update on mindfulness meditation as a self-help treatment for anxiety and depression*. Psychology research and behavior management, 2012.
https://www.ncbi.nlm.nih.gov/pmc/articles/PMC3500142/.

Francis, Bergogelio. Letter to Brazilians. "Message of Pope Francis for the Lenten Brother Campaign in Brazil." *Vatican.va*, 2014. https://www.vatican.va/.

Francis, Bergogelio, and Alicia von Stamwitz. *The Spirit of Saint Francis: Inspiring Words from Pope Francis*. Cincinnati, Ohio: Franciscan Media, 2015.

Francis, Giuliano Ferri, and Elio Sala. *The Prayer of St. Francis*. 2013. Print.

Frost, R. *Mending Wall by Robert Frost*. Poetry Foundation, 1914. https://www.poetryfoundation.org/poems/44266/mending-wall.

Gore, A., & Lewis, L. *Joy is an inside job!: and it's free!: 12 timeless secrets for abundance, radiant health and lifelong happiness*. Head2Heart, 2015.

Hall, David M. *The Abc's of Leadership: 26 Characteristics of More Effective Leadership*. Bloomington, Indianna: AuthorHouse, 2007.

Hari, J. *Everything You Think You Know About Addiction is Wrong*. TED, 2015. https://www.ted.com/talks/johann_hari_everything_you_think_you_know_about_addiction_is_wrong.

Hawn, M. *History of Hymns: 'Jesus, Joy of Our Desiring'*. Discipleship Ministries, 2020. https://www.umcdiscipleship.org/articles/history-of-hymns-jesus-joy-of-our-desiring.

John Paul II. "Fides et Ratio." The Holy See, 14 Sept. 1998, w2.vatican.va/content/john-paulii/en/encyclicals/documents/hf_jp_ii_enc_14091998_fides-et-ratio.html.

Lieberman, Matthew. *The Social Brain and Its Superpowers*. YouTube. TED video, 2013. https://www.youtube.com/watch?v=NNhk3owF7RQ.

Marie, B. A. *Grace Perfects Nature*. 2008, Catholicism.org. https://catholicism.org/grace-perfects-nature.html.

MacLaren, Ian. *Afterwards and Other Stories*. N.p.: CreateSpace Independent Publishing Platform, 2017.

May, G. G. *Addiction and Grace: Love and Spirituality in the Healing of Addictions*. HarperSanFrancisco, 2007.

S. Bonaventura: *Legendae duae de Vita S. Francisci*. Quarachi, 1898. (English translation by Miss Lockhart, Washbourne, 1898.)

ThoughtCo. *Learn the Words to the Catholic Prayer, 'Come, Holy Spirit'*. Learn Religions, Aug. 25, 2020, learnreligions.com/come-holy-spirit-prayer-542615.

Todd, Rev. Wilmer L. "The Disposition of the Receiver Determines the Message Received." The Lafourche Gazette, March 3, 2020. https://www.lafourchegazette.com/columns/what_a_life/the-disposition-of-the-receiver-determines-the-message-received/article_18be4266-60b5-5ede-94b0-b74e4d595f3e.html.

Turton, W.H. "Thou, Who at thy First Eucharist didst Pray", Hymnary.org, 2007. hymnary.org/text/lord_who_at_thy_first_eucharist_didst_pr.

VonSchlegel, Katharina. "Be Still My Soul". Amazing Hymns, 2021. https://amazinghymns.com/be-still-my-soul.

Wintz, J. *Saint Francis' Prayer before the Crucifix*. Franciscan Media, 2020. https://www.franciscanmedia.org/franciscan-spirit-blog/saint-francis-prayer-before-the-crucifix.

Wong, C. *The Cry for and the Cry of Humility*. Salt&Light, 2019. https://saltandlight.sg/devotional/the-cry-for-and-the-cry-of-humility/.

Check out Sacred Heart Healing Ministries for in-person and online retreats, parish missions, and more resources for your journey!
www.sacredhearthealingministries.com